D1381197

SUV

SUV

The World's Greatest

Sport Utility Vehicles

Giles Chapman

First published 2005 by Merrell Publishers Limited

Head office
81 Southwark Street
London SE1 0HX

New York office
49 West 24th Street, 8th Floor
New York, NY 10010

www.merrellpublishers.com

Text copyright © 2005 Giles Chapman
Design and layout copyright © 2005 Merrell Publishers Limited
Illustrations copyright © 2005 the copyright holders; see p. 240

All rights reserved. No part of this publication may be reproduced,
stored in any retrieval system or transmitted, in any form or
by any means, electronic, mechanical, photocopying, recording
or otherwise, without the prior permission in writing from
the publisher.

Publisher Hugh Merrell
Editorial Director Julian Honer
US Director Joan Brookbank
Sales and Marketing Manager Kim Cope
Sales and Marketing Executive Nora Kamprath
Managing Editor Anthea Snow
Project Editor Claire Chandler
Junior Editor Helen Miles
Art Director Nicola Bailey
Junior Designer Paul Shinn
Production Manager Michelle Draycott
Production Controller Sadie Butler

British Library Cataloguing-in-Publication Data:
Chapman, Giles
SUV : the world's greatest sport utility vehicles
1.Sport utility vehicles
I.Title
629.2'2042

ISBN 1 85894 274 8

Designed by Martin Lovelock
Picture research by Helen Stallion
Copy-edited by Christine Davis

Printed and bound in China

Jacket, front (clockwise from top): Porsche Cayenne (see pp. 220–23);
BMW X3 (see pp. 184–87); Lincoln Navigator (see pp. 204–207);
Volvo XC90 (see pp. 212–15)

Jacket, back (clockwise from top left): Toyota Land Cruiser
(see pp. 44–47); Nissan Patrol (see pp. 104–107); Willys Jeep
(see pp. 32–35); Mitsubishi Pajero/Shogun (see pp. 108–11);
Land Rover Freelander (see pp. 180–83)

Introduction 9

The World's Greatest Sport Utility Vehicles **30**

Glossary 234

Index 238

Picture Credits 240

Contents

Recognize this? It's an International Scout, introduced in 1960 and the first vehicle in the world to use the "sport utility" tag. So, in many respects, it's the foundation of the entire SUV genre.

Introduction

Twenty-first-century civilizations love acronyms. The more difficult to define the phrase is that they compress, the more the acronyms catch hold. So the sonorous utterance "SUV" has become a convenient catchall for a spectrum of motor vehicles that draw their design inspiration from a wide variety of sources and, yet, are difficult to pigeonhole. SUV stands for "sport utility vehicle," and after being absorbed in the study of the genre for more than a year, I understand this written form—with "sport" in the singular—to be the worldwide standard. Superficially, it's an easy one to understand as, surely, any vehicle to which it is applied is a combination of utilitarianism—evidently a tough and no-nonsense approach to the carriage of cargo mixed with passengers—and sportiness. But not the sportiness found in a "sports car"—a

A Willys "General Purpose" vehicle tackles some extremely demanding terrain; the combination of four-wheel drive, lightness, fitness for purpose, and vaguely carlike proportions made it a winner.

term, incidentally, that has never been alternatively expressed as "sport car." Sports cars are so called because of their derivation from pure racing cars, and the allusion is to the competitive sport of one driver competing with another to win a speed event.

The "sport" in "sport utility" refers to outdoor activities in which human beings take on nature, rather than each other, and use their wits and cunning to conquer it. Such activities encompass anything from fishing, shooting, and hunting to rock-climbing, kayaking, and field-walking. To this category, although significantly different in its reward since it involves no actual predation or exercise, can be added driving off-road. I can say this because the first car manufacturer actually to adopt the "sport utility" tag was International Harvester, with its Scout aimed purely and simply at American outdoorsmen.

However, the lines between "sport" and "sports" have blurred lately, and indeed have been blurred by carmakers who want to imbue large, heavy, and cheap-to-make vehicles with the "sporty" image associated with the heartbeat-raising pastimes of athletics. It's a kind of flattery cleverly used in the same way that strongly branded sports equipment has become everyday apparel for wearers who are obviously out of shape. An obese person wearing a tracksuit tries to convey the image that he or she is really an athlete underneath all that flab; likewise, a "sporty" SUV driver, while seated at the steering wheel, listening to the radio, and eating a doughnut, takes on—in his or her own mind at least—the clear-headed, oxygen-pumping, rippling physique that the driver of an ordinary family car lacks. And that image, of course, is very useful for marketing.

However, SUV is also a rather nebulous term, with no commonly agreed, legal definition. Outside the USA, an SUV is simply a variation on the standard passenger car, but in the United States an SUV is often classified as a "light truck" if it has a gross weight (that is, its total weight when fully loaded with passengers and cargo) of 8500 lb. (3856 kg), and if it is demonstrably "an automobile capable of off-highway operation." Light trucks are also supposed to be "automobiles that are not passenger automobiles"; they can carry passengers, but that is not supposed to be their primary purpose. By qualifying as a light truck, an SUV enjoys a more favorable tax regime

One of the pioneering passenger cars with four-wheel drive was this 1909 FWD hailing from Wisconsin, although its primitive power transmission technology was not widely adopted.

in the USA than an equivalently powered sedan or station wagon. So, suddenly, from a buyer perspective, that "utility" epithet is almost more important than the "sport" one.

Of course, those people who don't use or understand the SUV tag may also recognize such vehicles as "off-roaders," "four-wheel drives," or "four-by-fours." This is because, due to historical reasons as well as legislative ones, SUVs almost always have a high ground clearance and power transmitted through all four wheels so that they can traverse nontarmac terrain such as mud, sand, and undergrowth.

That is the matrix formed around the SUV term, but what of the vehicles themselves? The salute to the world's fifty landmark designs in this book—from the pioneers right the way through to the very latest—kicks off with the Willys Jeep since that was the first nimble four-wheel drive vehicle close to the scale of a conventional car and the bedrock on which the slowly (at first) evolving SUV formula was created. It certainly was not the first four-wheel drive production car: among those was the FWD of 1909, a large American car that, thanks to a patented double-Y universal joint, gave power to the front-steered wheels as well as the back ones. Even then, there were earlier pioneers, such as the prototype Löhner-Porsche of 1899, which offered four-wheel drive by the means of an electric motor fitted to the center of each of its quartet of wheels.

It is with the Dutch firm Spyker, however, that the system of power transmission to front and rear wheels via a transfer case and driveshafts is attributable, introduced in 1903. This is the system

An electric motor contained in the hub of each wheel of the experimental 1899 Löhner-Porsche made it the first automobile in the world with four-wheel drive, although only a handful were constructed, in Vienna, Austria.

intrinsic to the US Army's blueprint for an ideal small scout car that paved the way for the Willys Jeep's introduction in 1941, and it was configured so that drive to the front wheels could be disconnected. Thus, the vehicle could use rear-wheel drive only when driving along paved roads; this saved fuel and wear on components, both practical issues that weighed heavily on the minds of army strategists highly conscious of factors such as driving range and battlefield repairs. The Jeep's first imitator, the 1948 Land Rover, initially offered permanent four-wheel drive but soon also reverted to the versatility of manually selectable four-wheel drive.

The transformation of what had originally been a fighting vehicle into the SUVs of today began in 1948, and can be credited to the ingenuity of industrial designer Brooks Stevens and his brief to conceive cost-effective new outlets for Willys, the military Jeep's principal manufacturer, in peacetime. What is astonishing, in retrospect, is that a designer should have been involved at all,

The simple, boxy proportions of one of the earliest of Land Rovers, a 1948 Series I, concealed the fact that the vehicle had originally been designed around Jeep components. Moreover, the Land Rover was aimed fairly and squarely at the agricultural community.

The 1948 Willys Jeepster was shortlived, available for just three years between 1948 and 1951 and with fewer than 20,000 sold, but its Brooks Stevens-conceived design innovatively twisted military purposefulness to leisure intent for the first time.

since the destiny of much of the global automotive industry at that time was still in the hands of engineers and manufacturing experts rather than those who had an instinct for what customers might actually want to buy. With plenty of constraints, Stevens found innovative ways to tempt customers into buying a Willys Jeep as a practical car that could also be enjoyed as part of a "lifestyle" (not that such a term existed then). His initial designs, including the Jeepster, were actually commercial failures; Willys discovered that there were profits to be made in selling licenses to build the Jeep around the world, and in such mundane contracts as supplying the US Mail. However, after a decent breathing space, during which "ordinary" consumers became accustomed to the idea of a car that could "go anywhere," Jeep and Willys were back in 1962 with the Jeep Wagoneer. One of the first true motoring hybrids, it rolled the four-wheel drive freedom of the faithful old Jeep together with the expansive style and appointments of a typical station wagon. The Wagoneer may appear a motoring Goliath today, but it was a groundbreaker then.

Just four years later, the concept of adding four-wheel drive to a road car for reasons of safety and roadholding was heralded by the Jensen FF. Under a stunningly attractive rendering of Italian coachwork design, the FF offered phenomenal grip as each of its wheels hugged the road. Another sales disaster, the FF nonetheless inspired Subaru and later Audi to endow outwardly conventional car designs with light off-road capability and surefooted on-road handling. Buyers loved the Subaru Leone and Audi quattro because they were ordinary cars with extraordinary capabilities. Off-road vehicles from Jeep, Land Rover, Ford, General Motors, Toyota, and Nissan, meanwhile, continued to offer great gusto in tough off-road conditions but poor on-road driving characteristics and, in some cases, due to their tall stature in order to offer the requisite ground clearance and also roomy occupant accommodation, poor stability if driven without care. Separate chassis and rigid axles were excellent for crossing boulder-strewn riverbeds but offered appalling comfort for long drives on the turnpike, the superhighway, or anything in between.

The Jeep Wagoneer (this is actually a 1974 Wagoneer-based Cherokee model, the first Jeep with that name) was the first SUV designed from the ground up for the role, mixing the legendary Jeep go-anywhere capability with station-wagon friendliness.

The key vehicles that changed the SUV scene forever are the 1984 Jeep Cherokee and the 1994 Toyota RAV4. The former did away with a separate chassis but maintained the straight-lined body architecture that buyers had come to revere, to create a car that was ruggedly handsome yet at the same time safe to drive even by the most inept motorist. The latter, meanwhile, adopted softened, suggestive SUV contours and merely added them to a conventional passenger car floorpan that just happened to have four-wheel drive availability and large wheels. From these two, the modern SUV has emerged as a car that offers the two key features that buyers deem absolutely crucial— a high-seated, commanding driving position, and the comfort zone of four-wheel drive, for inclement weather and the odd diversion on to a rutted farm track—but has done away with the girder-like structure that, while marvelous for those who need a vehicle for genuine "off-highway" tasks, seriously hampers on-highway enjoyment.

There is some confusion among both customers and industry about the nomenclature used to describe the systems of giving power to every wheel. "Four-wheel drive" and "all-wheel drive" mean, literally, exactly the same thing, but as far as the automotive community is concerned there is a crucial difference. Four-wheel drive is accepted as meaning a manually engaging, part-time system in which the vehicle uses two-wheel drive most of the time but can be switched to four as and when conditions demand. All-wheel drive, by contrast, is taken to mean a permanently engaged or else automatically engaging four-wheel drive system; the driver doesn't choose the

The svelte Italian styling (by Carrozzeria Touring of Milan) of the 1966 Jensen FF luxury GT hid a true technical sensation: it was the first conventional production road car with four-wheel drive, as well as the first with antilock brakes, as standard.

four-wheel drive mode because either the car supplies it constantly or else computer-controlled, sensor-activated equipment turns it on at the point when it will be most beneficial to traction.

Obviously, all-wheel drive is far more user-friendly, and makes for a tidier cabin design because no mode selector is necessary. Almost all conventional passenger cars now have all-wheel drive where an option of four driven wheels is available (the Subaru Justy and Ford Tempo were among the last vehicles with selectable systems). Today, most new, smaller SUVs offer all-wheel drive too—a move that, once again, is allying the driving experience more closely with that of the conventional cars in which most people learn to drive. Such a system is civilizing, some might say sanitizing, the SUV for the widest possible market appeal but, on the other hand, there is little evidence that a permanent system diminishes off-road capability. Both the Range Rover and the Hummer H1 have offered full-time all-wheel drive from the outset, and they are regarded as among the finest off-highway vehicles ever designed.

In contrast to the unsuccessful Jensen FF, Subaru's 1973 Leone wagon added four-wheel drive to conventional family cars and brought it to the market at an affordable price; the styling might have been textbook mediocre, but the Leone's capabilities—as seen here— were astonishing.

The Audi quattro, introduced in 1980, broke new ground in adding four-wheel drive and a turbocharger to the compact sports coupé; its tremendous roadholding and phenomenal rallying success made it a turning point in Audi's fortunes.

This is not the place to debate the merits of the various transmission systems, however. This book is concerned with how the SUV looks today and how it got that way. By 2005, moreover, the proliferation of subspecies with SUV styling has left the rarefied arena of the motor show concept circuit and arrived at showrooms across the world.

Until the mid-1980s, SUVs uniformly possessed a straight-edged design aesthetic, usually a "two-box" van profile in which there was one smaller "box" to contain the power unit and another, larger one tacked on behind, where passengers and luggage were housed. The Mercedes G-Wagen, the Mitsubishi Pajero, and the Jeep Cherokee are all typical. The slightest hint of compound curvature was deemed out of the question, so much so that the pioneer of the mini-MPV, the Daihatsu Feroza/Sportrak of 1988, was merely a shrunken version of the traditional straight-lined, four-square, full-size designs.

A softening of this discipline finally came about with the Toyota RAV4 of 1994, the Isuzu VehiCROSS of 1997, and the BMW X5 of 1999. Although all offered decent amounts of utility, these vehicles finally assimilated the "buggy" look of the mid-1960s, when Californian enthusiasts created wide-tracked, low-slung plastic vehicles for racing across sand dunes. The apotheosis of these cars was the Meyers Manx, a design by Bruce Meyers, which like most others used all the components of a wrecked Volkswagen Beetle to bring it to life, since it was sold in home-build kit form. The Manx, in side profile, possesses the classic cartoon "dog-bone" shape, a stick representing the doorless cockpit and a knob on each end being the fat wheel and its embracing mudguard. It was this basic shape that provided the flared-out-looking "cushion" on which the new breed of 1990s SUVs appeared to ride, while adding station wagon- or van-like upper sections. The Manx, incidentally, does not merit a separate entry in this book for the simple fact that it was a car for carefree sport only, with no utilitarian element to its character. It is, nonetheless, an extremely important influence on the SUV.

In recent years the crossbreed of various car types with the SUV has been eagerly adopted as manufacturers have sought to bring the SUV in from the cold and make it a logical choice for any

As if to demonstrate its brilliant packaging, a Jeep Cherokee fits with ease into a Le Shuttle train bound for the Channel Tunnel. The Cherokee, introduced in 1984, did away with a separate chassis for better stability, fuel economy, and on-road manners, and for many people now represents the archetypal "Jeep."

Toyota created the RAV4 in 1994 after realizing the vast majority of buyers wanted four-wheel drive and a commanding driving position but were otherwise satisfied with "normal" road cars; hence, under those buggy-ish lines, it's a conventional road car much like a Toyota Camry.

motorist, not just those with a real—or imagined—use for a large four-wheel drive vehicle. The most dramatic transformation has been that of the Lexus RX300, which has been changed from a fundamentally station-wagon shape into something of a high-riding five-door coupé, while the Infiniti FX45, BMW X3, and Volkswagen Touareg have adopted sporty hatchback looks that have been scaled up to fit the SUV proportion. We have yet to see the SUV ethos expressed as a two-door, low-roof coupé (except as the Mitsubishi Pajero Evolution 2+2 concept in 2002), a conventional four-door sedan with a separate rear luggage trunk, or even a full convertible, but these iterations are doubtless waiting in the wings for the right launch opportunity.

Indeed, as I was writing this, a press release arrived from Mazda containing details of the MX-Crossport, a concept show car that the company exhibited at Detroit's North American International Auto Show in January 2005. The Crossport has the huge wheels and bulging fenders to contain them that are *de rigueur* on most SUVs these days, but the upper portion of the car is as

sleek, sculptural, and sensuous as any desirable sports sedan. Its low roofline with a narrowing side window aperture would not look out of place on an exotic Italian supercar, while the dramatic, five-spoke alloy wheels are derived from those of the Mazda RX-01, a prototype sports car of the mid-1990s. The Crossport emanated from Mazda's studio in Hiroshima and is the work of chief designer Iwao Koizumi. In Koizumi's words: "Our goal was to design a crossover that transcends the existing categories of SUVs and crossovers and steps into the realm of the sports car. We want to let people experience the world of sports cars every time they get behind the wheel. The cockpit has also been designed to perfectly match the powerfulness of the exterior design."

The MX-Crossport is certainly a finely executed example of up-to-the-minute, all-bases-covered car styling. But is it really what people want? A large number of current US-built SUVs stick with their overtly masculine, boxy looks because that is what the marketplace demands, and they are loath to desert their most loyal customers by trying to force perception changes on them. Rick Aneiros is a Detroit design executive with thirty-four years of experience working within Chrysler and its subsidiaries. Today he is vice president of Jeep and Truck Design within DaimlerChrysler, and the Jeep design studio complex he oversees has a dozen designers working full-time on future

The chiseled contours of the Range Rover—this is a four-door model dating from around 1984—made it a work of art in the eyes of the Louvre, and an object of lofty snob appeal for the many countryfolk who started to use the high-riding cars around town.

The unremittingly militaristic Hummer H1 finds a few idiosyncratic civilian customers each year, but the lure of the Hummer brand was cannily recognized by General Motors, which acquired it in 2000 and has since launched the H2 with H1 design cues diluted for a wider market.

production models and design concepts. Nonetheless, he is acutely aware of customer expectation: "In America, Jeep is SUV just like Kleenex is a face towel," he says. "The industry definition of an SUV might be shifting and the center of gravity is now more of a balance between on- and off-road performance. But any Jeep must always be the most capable off-road vehicle in its segment, and that's even if the customer only ventures off the highway just once in a lifetime. That is core." However, in the mind of the customer, any new Jeep in the accepted idiom must look just like, well, a Jeep. Aneiros continues:

That means traditional boxy, rectilinear, formal. We fail if someone says: "Hey, look, that can't be a Jeep!" When the CJ was changed to become the Wrangler and lost its identity, that was soon recognized as a mistake, and even the "fanned-out" grille of the second-generation Grand Cherokee was not liked so much by customers as the more straight-sided original, which is why we're changing it back. Customers say, time and again, "Look, whatever you do, don't change the look of my Jeep." Fortunately, our designers love the tradition of that culture—they want to leave their mark on it.

Hence the Jeep Rescue concept of 2004, a conservative and square-lined wagon redolent of the military vehicles that the word "Jeep" sums up in even the most car-illiterate minds the world over. "That's a viable car for us," says Aneiros. "It's robust, it reflects the duty cycle of activities like towing, and we could almost make it from components that already exist." However, he also hints at a new direction for a lighter, more economical Jeep, maybe something not unlike the three-seater Treo fun car shown at the Tokyo Motor Show in 2003. "We couldn't make a viable business proposition for that in the end," he continues, "partly because it didn't match American tastes, which tend to be along the lines of 'larger is better.' But we intend to create another branch of the Jeep brand which will venture out; we feel we can explore the Jeep envelope and reach out much further."

In the years to come, however, predicting what sort of designs customers will desire may be the easy part for manufacturers of SUVs. With the rapid move of the sport utility vehicle away from

The Mitsubishi Pajero, here in its MkII disguise, is a great example of Japanese manufacturers' ability to take the most appealing SUV elements and package them in cars with global appeal; the Pajero, moreover, has an enviable motor sport record.

its traditional domains of farms, country estates, and parks—in addition to its role in frontline services like fire brigades, coastguards, and police forces—and into the suburban driveways of "ordinary" car owners, has come a vocal backlash against the genre. Few drivers, apart from those whose country homes lie at the end of cinder tracks, or for whom the local, mountainous roadscape is a wintry one for a large part of the year, have an actual need for a trucklike four-wheel drive vehicle. The very different dynamics that traditional SUVs exhibit compared to conventional sedans or station wagons have also resulted in a sometimes poor understanding of how to drive them. To some people, their excesses of power, metal, resource consumption, and demonstrable, overbearing superiority—maybe even metaphorical bullying of other road users—are intolerable. There are powerful municipal voices in European cities including Paris and London who seek revenge; in the USA, objectors have examined local bylaws to find ancient loopholes through which the driving of SUVs can be forbidden, while moralizers paste "What would Jesus drive?" stickers

This is an Isuzu VehiCROSS; launched in 1997, it's a novel amalgam of traditional off-roader and beach buggy-inspired styling, and is also notable for making the transition from motor show concept car to showroom product, albeit one that was virtually handmade in small numbers.

on the bumpers of Ford Explorers. In the Middle East, SUVs are accused of "Toyota-ization" (a term coined by Oxford University professor of geography Andrew Goudie), which refers to a destructive trail that Toyota Land Cruisers and their ilk leave on the desert surface, leading to an increase in dust storms.

Detractors across the world speak fiercely of banning four-wheel drives and clobbering the "school-run moms" who clog up streets with oversize off-roaders. But the question of how this might be translated meaningfully into legislation is addressed only vaguely. As this book illustrates, SUVs can take all sorts of forms, and the slightly enlarged station-wagon profile of, say, a Subaru Forester has never raised much ire anywhere. Then there is the issue of economical gas–electric hybrids. The Toyota Prius, voted European Car of the Year for 2005 in its second-generation form, is the epitome of modern motoring saintliness, but it's notable that the first hybrid vehicle from an American manufacturer (the 43-mpg/18-kpl Ford Escape, which can switch to its pollution-free electric motive unit in cities) is an SUV. In what way would it be fair to banish this earnest vehicle from an urban environment and yet allow in, say, an ill-serviced, ten-year-old Honda Accord?

The main attraction of SUVs to mud-averse urban dwellers is, really, ride height. Four-wheel drive is almost an accidental legacy of being descended from something that had to have this feature for good ground clearance. Almost every city driver of an SUV will immediately cite commanding visibility as the most important attribute and the main reason/excuse why he or she bought such a vehicle. Rarely referred to is the fact that this physical elevation (rather like the

The Lexus RX300, quite apart from broadening the spectrum of "premium" SUVs on offer, has in its second-generation iteration shown here transformed the SUV into a high-riding "crossover" fastback sedan for the first time.

The concept version of the Mazda Crossport is at the cutting edge of SUV "crossover" in 2005, with upper body architecture that would not be out of place on a sleek sports sedan, yet riding on a big-wheeled, pumped-up base that communicates its off-road aplomb.

sedan chairs that, thanks to the four-heel drive of two uncomplaining servants, carried noble people through the rubbish-strewn streets of seventeenth-century London) is also the key to a feeling of superiority spiked heavily with invulnerability. SUV drivers look down on people, but they also "look down on" people. I briefly owned a Range Rover while living in London, and to drive it around the city was, of course, to lord it over others. It would be dishonest of me to say there wasn't something alarmingly seductive about this. You get resentment from other road users; you just don't care, but it's hardly admirable.

Interestingly, thirty-five years ago ownership of a Range Rover indicated that you were almost certainly from the landed gentry: the vehicle was a symbol of the landowning *status quo*. Redistribution of wealth, equal opportunities, and the so-called "classless" society have since turned tables. An SUV is now the biggest, tallest, and generally most ostentatious motoring way to say that you've got money and status, and that you are not about to be cowed into being modest about it.

It's easy to understand the desire for the elevated driving position and, possibly, the need for all the wheels to be powered. Furthermore, if SUVs are to be banned from cities for sheer reasons of harmony between socioeconomic groupings, surely any Mercedes-Benz, Bentley, or Ferrari should be outlawed too. On the other hand, perhaps some sort of controlling influence needs to be exerted by a responsible automotive industry on the design aesthetic of SUVs to curb the intimidation and sense of superiority that they exude.

A more pertinent reason for the growth of SUV ownership should perhaps be our aging society. With aching limbs and stiff joints, it's a lot easier to step into an SUV than adopt the twisting, stooping action needed to get into a typical conventional car. And the same rationale could certainly be applied to any adult who has the backbreaking task of maneuvering small children in and out of car seats. In this respect, we might consider the case of the new Ford Freestyle: each member of the team that came up with this inoffensive, relatively low-lined, four-wheel drive station wagon/SUV hybrid donned so-called "third-age suits" as part of the research process. These suits gave them an awareness of how it feels to move like an elderly person, while goggles were worn to give the impression of having cataracts. Hampered with these impediments, the designers came up with an SUV-style product that was easy to access, with controls and features that were simple to comprehend and operate.

There is also the intangible issue of so-called "security," a word that has been hijacked recently by politicians and turned into a universal concern. Airline pilots no longer announce that things are done for "your comfort and safety" but for "your safety and security." Likewise, car buyers have come to believe that "security" is an important benefit—and one mentioned in the sales literature

The 2004 Jeep Rescue concept is nonetheless, according to the company's Rick Aneiros, "a viable car for us"—by which he means boxy, rectilinear, almost ready to be built from existing components, and sympathetic to customer expectations.

for virtually every model—that SUVs have over and above other cars. The "parapet mentality" conveyed in much SUV marketing certainly leads some people to feel that they are more secure in an SUV than in other cars, but how can such security be objectively tested? Many, no doubt, are parents who would claim only to be doing the best for their families.

American satirist P.J. O'Rourke, writing in his usual biting manner in London's *Sunday Times*, got straight to some of the uncomfortable points about the appeal of the SUV to US drivers:

> We're big people from a big country. We like our elbowroom so much we carry it around with us. ... An SUV is very safe in a collision—for me anyway, because I drive one. ... Americans demand convenient parking. Conveniently, SUVs can be (crunch) parked anywhere. ... When all the oil is gone the people of the Middle East will be able to go back to being "Sand French." And the sooner America's SUVs use up that oil, the sooner global warming can be halted ...

Such is the entrenchment that car designers of the early twenty-first century face, although that should only heighten the challenge for them. It seems clear, however, that the upcoming generation of designers, particularly those who immerse themselves in lateral thinking and strategic vision, accept with some degree of reluctance the need to create SUVs. Manufacturers' spokespeople bubble over with enthusiasm when explaining the potential market possibilities for

"We're big people from a big country," wrote P.J. O'Rourke, and the Jeep Treo concept shown in 2003 didn't chime in with the US consumer's ethos of "bigger is better." But a new branch of the Jeep brand is currently being planned to take it beyond its traditional realm.

SUVs, but when I recently met with a group of postgraduate car design students at London's Royal College of Art to discuss SUV design, many of them could barely disguise their disdain for an automotive type that is intended for one sphere (off-road) but almost universally used in another (on). It's the complete opposite of one of the most basic tenets of product design—that of form following function—and is an uncomfortable reminder to car design recruits of the sometimes counterintuitive nature of the industry they're entering. In a show of some thirty hands (from those aged at least twenty-five) at the RCA, only one student, a Canadian, admitted to actually owning an SUV, and even he deplored many aspects of the design of the vehicle itself.

But whether designers, campaigners, or drivers like it or not, the SUV has evolved over six decades, is here to stay, and to many people represents the absolute cutting edge of car design. This book analyzes in detail the design of the fifty most influential SUVs to have hit the road—and often the mud—so far. I make no apologies for any omissions because there are as many clones in the SUV sphere as in any other in the automotive industry; a detailed breakdown of every single design change in, say, the entire life story of the Chevrolet Blazer would soon become dull to anyone but a fanatic and anyway is available elsewhere, most notably on the Web. This book is so far the only one in which the design of SUVs has been seriously considered and explained. And as the SUV today sits atop a mountain of controversy like no other car type before it, I hope it leaves you better informed as to how these extraordinary vehicles have come to look the way they do.

This is the Ford Freestyle, an SUV-like car expressly designed with older people in mind. So, the easy-to-access vehicle height was matched with user-friendly controls and features to make car travel a joy for those with stiff joints and cataracts.

32 **Willys Jeep**

36 **Willys Jeep Station Wagon/Jeepster**

40 **Land Rover Series I to Defender**

44 **Toyota Land Cruiser**

48 **Alfa Romeo 1900M • Fiat Campagnola**

52 **International Scout**

56 **Jeep Wagoneer**

60 **Ford Bronco**

64 **Chevrolet/GMC Suburban**

68 **Mini Moke • Citroën Mehari • Renault Rodeo • Volkswagen 181**

72 **Savio Jungla • Fissore Scout • Moretti MidiMaxi**

76 **Range Rover**

80 **Suzuki Jimny • Daihatsu Taft • Daihatsu Terios**

84 **Chevrolet Blazer**

88 **Subaru Leone**

92 **Monteverdi Safari • Lamborghini LM**

96 **Volkswagen Iltis • Mercedes-Benz G-Wagen**

100 **Matra Rancho**

104 **Nissan Patrol/Terrano**

108 **Mitsubishi Pajero**

112 **Isuzu Trooper/Amigo**

116 **Lada Niva**

120 **Jeep Cherokee/Grand Cherokee**

124 **Rayton Fissore Magnum**

128 **Jeep Wrangler**

The World's Greatest

132 **Fiat Panda 4x4 • Volkswagen Golf Country • Peugeot 505 Dangel**
136 **Ford Explorer**
140 **Land Rover Discovery**
144 **Daihatsu Feroza**
148 **Suzuki Vitara/X-90**
152 **SsangYong Musso • Kia Sportage • Kia Sorento • SsangYong Rexton**
156 **Isuzu VehiCROSS**
160 **Mercedes-Benz M-Class**
164 **Honda CR-V/HR-V/Pilot**
168 **Toyota RAV4**
172 **Nissan Terrano II • Ford Maverick**
176 **Subaru Forester**
180 **Land Rover Freelander**
184 **BMW X3/X5**
188 **Audi allroad • Renault Megane Scenic 4x4**
192 **Pontiac Aztek**
196 **Hyundai Santa Fe/Tuscon**
200 **Dodge Durango**
204 **Lincoln Navigator • Cadillac Escalade/Cadillac SRX**
208 **Lexus RX300**
212 **Volvo XC90**
216 **Hummer H1**
220 **Porsche Cayenne • Volkswagen Touareg**
224 **Nissan Murano • Infiniti FX45**
228 **Chrysler Pacifica**

Sport Utility Vehicles

Willys Jeep

In 1941, when Willys-Overland started making Jeeps in its Ohio factory, there was no such thing as an "SUV." The first Jeeps weren't really sold at all; they were issued. The main "customers" were the Allied Forces seeking to restore peace to a battle-scarred Europe during the Second World War, and every ounce of design effort went toward that resolute goal.

The vehicle was conceived in 1938 by the US Army to replace the motorbikes used to carry messages between US Army units. Only a fraction of the wartime Jeeps would stay in the USA, however, as hundreds of thousands of America's "General Purpose" vehicles were dispatched to Europe.

By the end of 1940, three American motor manufacturers had responded to the military brief: the American Bantam Car Company, with its Blitz Buggy proposal; Willys-Overland, with the Quad; and Ford, with the General Purpose, or GP.

Bantam delivered three prototypes to the army in September 1939. Each weighed 1275 lb. (578 kg), but they proved flimsy under test. Willys-Overland's vice president of engineering, Delmar "Barney" Roos, meanwhile, proposed his "mosquito car." Colonel Rutherford, chief of the Planning Section of the General Staff, liked this when he saw it in December 1939, and Willys-Overland rapidly developed it into a light, maneuverable, and powerful vehicle capable of carrying troops and weapons. Ford's was an unremarkable third choice.

In June 1940, army officers visited the Bantam factory to examine a second proposal, which was again deemed too light and was rejected. However, in July 1940, when the army surveyed 135 manufacturers for rapid delivery of 70 vehicles—each weighing 1300 lb. (590 kg), with a 660-lb. (299-kg) payload, an engine giving 85 lb./ft. (115 Nm) of torque, and an 80-in. (2032-mm) wheelbase—Bantam alone promised total delivery in 75 days. Willys bid 120 days. So Bantam won the tender by default.

However, Roos added a note to his unsuccessful Willys bid, stating "no substantial vehicle" was possible at 1300 lb. He explained

The Willys MB, opposite, the classic warhorse, had a birth beset by complex design wrangling, but its blueprint was unadulterated for civilian versions such as the CJ5, below.

this to Major H.J. Lawes, purchasing and contracting officer for the US Army's military base at Camp Holabird, Maryland, and Lawes suggested that Willys-Overland build its own pilot model to prove it. Ford, the other bid loser, was also given this tip-off; the government wanted as much design choice as possible. However, in September 1940, Bantam designer Karl Probst unveiled a third prototype called the "Blitz Buggy." Willys engineers, including Roos, could hardly believe its agility, stamina, and compactness, and they returned to their headquarters in Toledo, Ohio, determined to outdo him.

Two Willys-Overland vehicles were subsequently delivered to Camp Holabird, on November 11, 1940. Named the "Quad," they had selectable two- or four-wheel drive, and one boasted four-wheel steering. The army was impressed, but Bantam was livid: the Quad looked identical to Probst's Blitz Buggy because the army had given Willys (and Ford) free access to Bantam blueprints.

The Willys MA, above, was selected as the standard military vehicle design by the US Army in 1941. Note the raised position of the headlights, compared to their familiar position on this 1950 model, right.

The final Bantam, Willys, and Ford prototypes were, therefore, very similar. The 2030-lb. (921-kg) Bantam vehicle exceeded the original 1300-lb. weight stipulation but was still lighter than the 2400-lb. (1089-kg) Willys. However, the Willys was the only one to meet and indeed exceed the army's power requirement, with the 105 lb./ft. (142 Nm) of torque from its gutsy "Go Devil" engine dwarfing Bantam's 83 and Ford's 85. Still, the US Army ordered 1500 vehicles from each maker for field tests, and acknowledged the 1300-lb. weight requirement as unrealistic by upping it to 2160 lb. (980 kg). Roos's team painstakingly lightened the Quad until eventually it was just 7 oz. (198 g) off this target. Delivery of the 4500 models began in June 1941, at which point the army decided to standardize one design, the Willys, with some Ford and Bantam features adopted too. In July 1941, Willys then won a contract for 16,000 vehicles, while later that year, the US Army ordered Willys-Overland to share its designs with Ford to boost production. During the Second World War, Willys-Overland and Ford together built 600,000 Jeeps, with Willys supplying 368,000—and tiny Bantam just 2675.

As Willys-Overland production rose, the name Jeep—the slurring of the acronym "GP," for General Purpose, but also, as "Eugene the Jeep," a popular, impish newspaper cartoon character in the Popeye strip—became synonymous with it, and soon became a universal term.

General George Marshall called the Jeep "America's greatest contribution to modern warfare." Indeed, the story of the Second World War is also the story of the Jeep's early years because after 1941 it served in every campaign as a litterbearer, machine gun-firing mount, reconnaissance vehicle, pickup truck, frontline limousine, ammunition bearer, wirelayer, and taxi.

But what of the Jeep's styling? Forget it: none had ever been envisaged. The front pressing with its nine vertical slats and circular cutouts for lights looks distinctive, but was nothing more than a compromise between cheapness and sturdiness. The metal front mudguards are just that, creased into shape on rudimentary

machinery, while the curved cutouts giving entry to the tub-like passenger area were only thus shaped so as not to catch a military boot or gunsight on maneuvers. And yet, although no one had time to ponder it then, the Jeep certainly had a style that was all its own.

WORLD'S MOST USEFUL VEHICLE
RUGGED, VERSATILE, DEPENDABLE
BIG PAYLOAD—60% OF CURB WEIGHT
OPTIONAL CANVAS TOPS OR METAL CABS
ECONOMICAL 4-CYLINDER ENGINE

Jeep UNIVERSAL
MODEL CJ-3B

Jeep 4-CYLINDER F-HEAD "HURRICANE" ENGINE

Positive exhaust valve rotation, cast-in-head intake manifolding, aluminum alloy pistons increase the life span of this remarkable engine—give you dependable performance, money-saving mileage and more maintenance-free service.

72 H.P. @ 4000 R.P.M.; 114 lbs. ft. Torque @ 2000 R.P.M.; Displacement 134.2cu. in.

WE HAVE A 'JEEP' VEHICLE FOR YOUR TOUGHEST JOB!

WILLYS MOTORS, INC.
WILLYS-OVERLAND EXPORT CORP.
TOLEDO, OHIO

Form No. 59-08

Printed in U.S.A.

After the Second World War the push of "Jeep" into civilian markets began in earnest, with the advertisement above being typical of the hard sell. Yet sales of military vehicles, right, were boosted by the Korean War.

Willys Jeep Station Wagon/Jeepster

A lucrative defense contract was one thing, but how could Willys-Overland possibly hope to sustain its Toledo plant after the Second World War?

The company's president, Charles Sorensen, calculated that Willys needed to sell 54,000 Jeeps annually to make a profit, but he knew he could not sell that many even in the medium term. Before the war the company had made low-priced family cars, but its body suppliers were now all contracted to rivals, and tooling up from scratch involved huge costs.

So Sorensen elected that, henceforth, Willys would be principally a maker of utility and commercial vehicles for which cheap, simple pressings (actually produced in a washing machine plant) were a positive advantage,

rather than trying to take on Ford and Chevrolet in cars. The foundation of this move was the military Jeep modified for civilian use with such additions as windshield wipers and the word "WILLYS" boldly stamped in the metal panel of the pickup tailgate—a practice since widely copied; the vehicle was painted in cheerful colors and was called the CJ2A Universal. Simultaneously, however, Sorensen hired one of the new breed of independent industrial designers to maximize the amount of product sophistication that Willys could squeeze from its scant resources.

Like his contemporaries Raymond Loewy and Walter Dorwin Teague, Wisconsin-based Brooks Stevens was transforming the way everyday objects in America looked—

everything from peanut butter jars to garden furniture and, of course, cars. These products silently preached a similar mantra: functional could also be beautiful. And Stevens was a master at achieving it. By the time he died in 1995, he had worked for 550 clients, with *Time* magazine declaring him "The seer that made Milwaukee famous."

With his fertile imagination, Stevens immediately came up with an idea: use the

With the enigmatic Jeep nose jutting out of a fake timber "cube," the Jeep Station Wagon, below, was something genuinely novel in 1946 America. Willys's advertising, opposite, squandered no chance to ram home the car's many benefits.

YOU GET MORE for your money in a Willys-Overland 'Jeep' Station Wagon . . . and at its new low price, it's a better buy than ever! You get a comfortable, smooth-riding passenger car, with inches more head-room and better visibility—18 to 50% more glass area—than any popular sedan. You also get a utility vehicle with seats easily removable to give huge load space. Let your Willys-Overland dealer take your family for a trial ride in this doubly-useful steel-body station wagon . . . top value in its field.

MORE Usefulness – MORE Economy – MORE Value

MORE luggage room—with seats in, 10 to 29% more usable carrying space than competitive sedans. Removing seats gives 98 cu. ft. of load space.

MORE practical for family or business use. Seats wipe clean with a damp rag. Interior paneling and slatted steel floor can be washed repeatedly.

MORE ease of handling, with quick steering action and better visibility . . . highly maneuverable in traffic . . . parks in 2 to 3 less feet with one turn.

ROAD TEST OF FUEL MILEAGE AT 40 MILES PER HOUR

JEEP' STATION WAGON 4 CYLINDER	
SEDAN A	
SEDAN B	
SEDAN C	
SEDAN D	

MORE mileage—road tests at 40 m.p.h. showed 4½ to 7 more miles per gallon than 4 popular standard sedans!

WILLYS–OVERLAND
'Jeep' Station Wagon
WITH 4 OR 6 CYLINDER ENGINE . . . OVERDRIVE STANDARD EQUIPMENT

sturdy CJ2A as the basis for a station wagon. In 1946, station wagons were largely scorned by urban-dwellers because they were bodied using wood and were associated with farmers and remote country life. Stevens's trick was to design a roomy, all-metal body that could then be painted to resemble a timber frame, and use a simplified, rear-wheel drive Jeep chassis. The Jeep Station Wagon was America's first all-steel wagon, albeit one that most people considered a commercial vehicle despite the fact that it had seven seats and a drop-down tailgate with lifting upper window section.

Was the Jeep Station Wagon the first sport utility vehicle? Well, a four-wheel drive and more powerful six-cylinder engine choices in 1949 added recognizable SUV elements to a neat and quite handsome design, with the enigmatic Jeep nose seemingly jutting out of the front of the station wagon "cube." Also, in 1951, Willys offered elaborate Jamaica, Grand Canyon, and Caribbean trim options in a groundbreaking if largely unsuccessful attempt to tap into the psyche of outdoors-oriented families.

Brooks Stevens also had another brainwave: the 1948 Jeepster, a spacious four-seater convertible that he called a "sports-phaeton" because it had no side windows. It seems remarkable that an Ohio truckmaker should have rubber-stamped such an adventurous project, but then Willys was carving out a new place for itself in the automotive pecking order, and Charles Sorensen was in the mood for innovation. From nose to windshield, the

The Jeep Jeepster, below, was a unique hybrid of sports car and warhorse. The Jeepster idea was briefly reprised in the early 1960s, opposite, although this time the car came with four-wheel drive.

Jeepster apes the Station Wagon, but the rear section is a flat-paneled open two-door tourer with Stevens's simple, squared-off styling and a robust, manually operated hood. It was a two-wheel drive vehicle, and really struck a different note on America's roads in the early 1950s.

Still, the rapidly garnered hicksville image of the Jeep (on June 13, 1950, Willys-Overland registered "Jeep" as its own international trademark) militated against both the Station Wagon and the Jeepster, practical and neat though they were. Both were dropped after 1951, and only 19,131 Jeepsters were sold. The Jeepster had been a sales flop, but Willys had the perfect excuse: the Korean War was in full swing, and military Jeep orders were flooding in once more. The SUV had, it seemed, come and gone.

Land Rover Series I to Defender

In Land Rover terms, it is entirely plausible to bracket together vehicles made in 1948 with those being built today. This is because the Defender range, still very much in production in Solihull in Britain's West Midlands, fulfills an almost identical role to its earliest ancestor, the Series I: a super-versatile, four-wheel drive workhorse—an essentially commercial or agricultural piece of equipment in which luxury and "fun" are absolutely secondary considerations.

On that design basis, basic Land Rovers are not SUVs. But their influence on the SUV world has been profound.

The first Land Rover would never have happened at all but for British government economic policy. In the grim, postwar industrial environment, raw steel was made a rationed commodity, with the biggest supplies allocated to manufacturers who could turn it into exportable goods. Sadly, most British cars were too feeble and unreliable for the former colonial export markets—Australia, Canada, and the USA—that lay in wait. Brothers Maurice and Spencer Wilks, who controlled the Rover Car Company, were among the few to respond to the challenge.

Moreover, Maurice Wilks owned a 250-acre (100-ha) farm on the Welsh island of Anglesey, where an ex-military Willys Jeep he'd bought as war surplus was doing sterling service as both a car and a tractor substitute. Whenever it broke under the strain, it was taken to Rover's Solihull factory for repairs. Rural Jeep ownership gave Wilks an idea: there was, literally, nothing else quite like it, so why not take the Jeep's outstanding off-road qualities and use them in a vehicle that farmers all over the world would long to own—and that Rover's underused plant could build?

The Wilks brothers spent the spring of 1947 on Anglesey, locked away in their own design think tank. By fall that year, their Solihull engineers had completed a prototype. "It must be along the lines of the Willys Jeep," Maurice Wilks instructed them, "but much more versatile, more useful as a power source, able to do everything." It will come as no surprise, then, that this vehicle looked very like a Willys; the 80-in. (2032-mm) wheelbase was the same because it actually used a Jeep body frame and

Betraying its shameless Jeep origins, the prototype Land Rover, below, was aimed at a slightly different market: the farmer. The tractor-like central driving seat failed to make it to production models, however.

axles. However, it had curved front mudguards that fully enclosed the front wheels, and also a single, central driving seat like a tractor. It was totally functional.

Rather than rationed steel, the vehicle's body panels were pressed from cheap and plentiful aluminum, which made it far lighter in weight. Four-wheel drive capability gave it exceptional ability on off-road terrain.

Rover's board approved the vehicle in September 1947, with some design changes, the main one being to insist on a conventional left- or right-hand drive steering position to broaden the appeal of what came to be christened the "Land Rover." The bodywork was

The Series I Land Rover gained square front fenders in order to lower manufacturing costs but retained the Jeep's close-set headlights, left. Customers were often affluent rather than agricultural, including former prime minister Sir Winston Churchill, above.

also altered, getting rid of the curved front fenders to replace them with cheaper-to-make square items. Tony Barker, chief engineer, recalled later: "We never thought about style—it just sort of happened." The profile of the Land Rover now resembled a collection of metal boxes on wheels. Within a year, pilot production was underway, and the vehicle was launched at the 1948 Amsterdam Motor Show. Prices started at a very cheap £450, but this model was so basic that it didn't even include a spare wheel. Power came from a four-cylinder 1.6-liter engine from the Rover 60.

The Wilks brothers were dumbfounded when, within two years, the Land Rover outsold their elegant Rover cars. By 1954, an incredible 100,000 had been built.

Notably, although Land Rovers were classed as commercial vehicles, Rover introduced a seven-seater station wagon body option in 1949. Although there was no diesel engine option until 1957, the design had already evolved: in 1954, to make for better handling on-road, the old Jeep wheelbase was extended to 86 in. (2184 mm), with a longer 107-in. (2718-mm) wheelbase also offered.

The 1961 Series II models, while offering deeper bodysides, which imparted a more solid look, carried on the SI's build system of aluminum panels on a separate steel chassis. In 1976, and long after the Wilks brothers had sold Rover, the one-millionth Land Rover was sold. By now it was a Series III, with headlights finally moved away from the in-grille position of the wartime Willys Jeep to the front fenders. And today's Defender (as the vehicles were renamed in 1990), despite being offered with 90-in. (2286-mm) or 110-in. (2794-mm) wheelbases, has hardly changed at all in concept, although it is now equipped with a less jarring coil-spring suspension, and plastic wheelarch extensions to accommodate broad modern tires.

With products such as the Range Rover, Discovery, and Freelander, Land Rover has now moved away from the uncomplicated, agricultural simplicity of its birth. Yet the Defender stands apart from this trend: its body peppered with rivet heads and its so-called styling as uncompromisingly angular as ever, it purveys the gruff image that all Land Rover owners, whether they acknowledge it or not, want a piece of.

Any styling on the short-wheelbase Series II Land Rover station wagon from 1966, below, was an accident of pure practicality, although the boxy contours are already very distinctive.

The Series III, left, finally saw its headlights moved to a conventional spot fronting the fenders. The 110, above, and its descendant the Defender, top, both seen here as long-wheelbase station wagons, remain remarkably faithful to the original Land Rover aesthetic.

Toyota Land Cruiser

The story of the Land Cruiser is also the story of the world's definitive off-road vehicle. The production tally alone proves it, with 4,095,975 built to the end of 2003, but switch on the television news and you get more proof. There they are in every battle-weary flashpoint around the world, Land Cruisers of every type and age, driven not only by United Nations peacekeepers but also by hooded gun-toters. There's scarcely a Jeep or a Land Rover in sight. At the same time, a scan of your own main street is sure to find a Land Cruiser fully loaded with children and groceries.

Toyota was the third company to tackle the idea of a "civilian" four-wheel drive vehicle, but it drove straight into controversy almost as effortlessly, when a prototype in the hands of Toyota test driver Ichiro Taira attacked the steps of the Fudo temple in Okazaki City for a publicity stunt in July 1951.

This was the launch event of the Toyota Model BJ, but it did not please Willys (nor its local assembly partner Mitsubishi) because not only was the vehicle a virtual replica of the Jeep Universal, down to its grille and bodyside profile, but Toyota had the temerity to call the BJ the "Toyota Jeep." The key difference was under the hood: the BJ had a 3.4-liter six-cylinder engine from a Toyota truck in, essentially, a car-derived chassis, these being the only elements that Toyota had at its disposal. The Toyota was both more powerful and more comfortable than a Willys Jeep.

Toyota had police forces in mind as principal customers, but they shunned the BJ. So instead, and no doubt with an eye on its competitors, Toyota decided to attack export markets with the car, especially Australia. For 1952, a redesign gave a longer, roomier, less Jeep-like body; there was an even bigger 3.9-liter engine and a four-speed gearbox. Meanwhile, to keep the lawyers at bay, Toyota managing director Hanji Umehara took a note out of Rover's book and renamed the BJ the Land Cruiser.

Full-scale production got underway in 1953, but it wasn't until 1958 that the Land Cruiser truly took on its own identity with the FJ25. In many ways the FJ25 constituted the evolutionary "softening" tidy-up that the Willys Jeep never received. Toyota kept the vestigial running boards and "open" style of mudguard essential for the dramatic approach angles needed to overcome rocky routes, but gave the Land Cruiser a simple rectangular grille incorporating round headlights at its ends, and a one-piece windshield. In addition, a fully enclosed van-type body was offered that, with windows (including distinctively curved windows in the rear body corners) and side-facing rear bench seats, made the Land Cruiser a touch more carlike. However, as Toyota acknowledges today, the company was pre-occupied at the time with the troublesome genesis of its Crown and Corona car ranges; as a result, the Land Cruiser design was handled by on-site engineers "working with little more than rulers and compasses."

With its new design independence from Jeep, the Land Cruiser was headed for the USA. Indeed, because the 1958 Crown sedan had bombed in North America, the Land Cruiser

Toyota's first Land Cruiser, the 1951 BJ, was a blatant Jeep copy in terms of appearance, although its construction was unusual in that it mated a car chassis with a powerful truck engine.

The 1958 FJ series, right, finally awarded
the Land Cruiser its own, distinctive
appearance, while the 1967 FJ55, below,
was properly styled. The FJ60 model,
above, featured separate front fenders
suggested in its decorative lines.

proved a sales lifeline; in 1962, for instance, Toyota sold 598 Land Cruisers there against just 113 normal passenger cars. In the aftermath of the Korean War, too, Toyota benefited enormously from American help; the US Army evaluated the Land Cruiser and advised Toyota on how it could be better made.

With continual small modifications, the Land Cruiser sailed on for decade upon decade before being replaced by the 70 Series in 1984. The 70 Series was better all round despite retaining a ladder-type chassis, but Land Cruiser enthusiasts knew an era had ended with the passing of the FJ40 series, a basic design that had lasted for twenty-nine years. They thought it had gone soft with such rudimentary updates as curved glass.

From a design standpoint, however, 1967 was a key year for the Land Cruiser. A more capacious Land Cruiser, the FJ35V, was originally conceived in the early 1960s mostly as a crewbus for building sites. Initially, an artless, elongated standard body did the job, but the 1967 FJ55 was a properly designed station wagon—the first divergence from the thoroughly utilitarian standard Land Cruiser, and created using design sketches, clay models, and a vague design notion that people might use one for leisure purposes. It received a straight-through fenderline for the first time, a feature that established itself as a separate mudguard at the front but turned into a waistline as it reached the front doors. The FJ55's visage, with headlights set close together, gives the car an innocently deranged expression; no wonder they nicknamed it "The Moose" in the USA.

A decade later, separate front mudguards were simply "suggested" by a crease on the FJ60 model's front fenders, one part of a package planned by chief engineer Hiroshi Oshawa to limit carefully changes to a highly successful product. The old-fashioned leaf springs, for example, were endlessly discussed but never changed because they gave the ultimate in off-road performance. By the 1980s, the Land Cruiser had a reputation to live up to, not establish, and a widened track was provided so the car was less likely to roll over when overloaded and driven on desert roads.

Today's Land Cruisers, like their forebears, do not set the design pace. They are contemporary but conservative, as their customers demand. The range is vast and fractured, encompassing 70 Series workhorses that are the direct descendants of the first Land Cruiser, "lifestyle" SUVs under the 90 Series Prado/ Colorado sub-brand, and an entire line of sophisticated, luxury-loaded 80 and 100 Series wagons. What they stand for, however, is a quality reputation garnered the hard way and evolved through nine distinct models.

The latest Land Cruiser, shown on these pages in three- and five-door forms, is the modern incarnation of an august motoring family, revered for its toughness, even if its design fails to stand out from the crowd.

Alfa Romeo 1900M - Fiat Campagnola

Consider sporting cars for a few moments and Italian cars will almost certainly roar into your thoughts. Surely, in view of all the engineering and design verve demonstrated by that country in the latter half of the twentieth century, Italy would have made a valuable contribution to the genesis of the SUV, at least in the "sport" sphere if not the "utility" one?

Maybe surprisingly, this is not the case. Not until the little-heralded arrival of the Rayton Fissore Magnum in 1984 was there a distinctively Italian SUV, and there has not been one since. However, it could have been so different, for both Alfa Romeo and Fiat were early entrants in the postwar off-road vehicle market.

The spur for this development was a lucrative postwar government contract for a Jeep-type vehicle for the Italian Army. Although the just-nationalized Alfa Romeo would have seemed the natural recipient of such an order, private-sector Fiat, which was controlled by the influential Agnelli family, was also able to muscle in, so there were two astonishingly similar answers to the same question. Indeed, both vehicles appear to have been identically codenamed AR51.

Deliveries of both Alfa's 1900M and Fiat's Campagnola began in 1951, and they closely followed the Willys template of front-mounted four-cylinder engine, four-wheel drive, and open bodywork. The only curvature is to the engine compartments: on the Alfa Romeo, the

side panels curve round to meet with a flat hood panel, and on the Fiat the hood curves down to meet with flat side panels. The Alfa has a rear wheelarch aperture of three straight lines, the Fiat a simple semicircle. Both, it must be said, resemble nothing so much as horsedrawn carts stuck on to the back of a basic truck nose, although the Alfa makes a stab at tradition with the crude outline of the Milanese company's heart-shaped radiator grille discernible in the punched-out slats of its nose panel.

An early Fiat Campagnola is shown on these pages with its doors "pinned back" for maximum access. Although devised for the armed forces, it was happily adopted by the Italian farming community.

The Alfa Romeo was the least successful, although it's unclear why. The car was based on the 1900 sedan, the first mass-production Alfa Romeo, but the company's automotive heritage was in fast and sometimes delicate sporting cars, rather than military workhorses. The vehicle used a detuned 65 bhp 1884 cc engine that, nonetheless, was a twin-cam unit with an alloy head, while four-wheel drive was permanent to the rear wheels and selectable for the fronts. The Italian Army took just 2050 vehicles, and Alfa Romeo sold an extra 155 cars, designated the AR52, to private buyers. The car was discontinued in 1953.

Fiat, by contrast, capitalized on its army deliveries. The engine was a 1901 cc four-cylinder giving 53 bhp but, in 1953, it added a 40 bhp diesel that made the vehicle a surefire hit with Italian farmers. A new model, the Campagnola A, in 1955 also spawned a new military model, the AR55, and later the AR59. The Campagnola remained a steady, rarely publicized Fiat mainstay until 1973, by which time 7783 diesel-engined examples, and 31,293 gas-engined ones, had been sold.

That was not the end of the Campagnola. Although still very much an agricultural or

industrial piece of machinery—rarely, if ever, considered a "car"—the Nuova Campagnola of 1974 carried on a, by now, long tradition of 4x4 Fiats. Underneath it had independent torsion bar suspension all round, and new engines, including a 2.5-liter diesel. In appearance, it had gone from antediluvian to generic 4x4, its perfectly semicircular wheelarches contrasting sharply with the ruler-straightness of all its other lines. From 1974 until 1979, the Campagnola was built entirely by renowned styling house Pininfarina, which, in 1976, introduced the first Campagnola with a metal roof. "It was tremendously important to us as a stimulus to further expansion on the manufacturing side," Sergio Pininfarina has said.

Fiat quietly retired the Campagnola in around 1986, probably feeling that this quirky niche product with its thirty-five-year history could have little use in the company's future plans. In retrospect, it was perhaps foolish to ditch what could now be a credible SUV heritage.

Rough and ready by usual Alfa Romeo standards, the 1900M used a 1900 car engine and reproduced (somewhat crudely) Alfa's traditional shield-shape grille at the front—but this four-wheel drive truck never really caught on.

The Fiat Campagnola A, below, was purely
a civilian vehicle, albeit still a very basic
one, but the Nuova Campagnola, above
and right, had neat styling and was built
by renowned coachbuilder Pininfarina.

International Scout

The introduction of the Scout is one of the most unlikely—and least recognized—success stories that the automotive industry has ever known. If you can imagine a truck and tractor manufacturer launching a new SUV today and, from scratch, snapping at Jeep's heels within twelve months, then that is exactly what happened in 1961.

Chicago's International Harvester Company had long been a maker of light trucks when it developed the theme into America's first domestic Willys Jeep competitor. At first glance, there would seem to be little of design merit to the Scout's cubic contours, but there is an honest simplicity to the vehicle. Its huge wheels are emphasized by flared wheelarches, and a hockeystick-like bodyside crease in the rear fender panels helps break up the massive side elevation, while the robust exterior door hinges and girder-like bumpers add a visual note of total indestructibility. There's an anonymity, too, that bestows the Scout with an image that's difficult to pigeonhole. Is the driver a site manager at a mine or, in fact, the owner of five thousand acres of country estate? The Scout would keep onlookers guessing.

The International Scout may have been based on a pickup, but that didn't prevent it from being the first four-wheel drive vehicle to chase leisure markets in 1960, as evidenced below. A Scout hardtop from the late 1970s is pictured on the opposite page.

International had an eye to what it recognized as a slowly expanding "recreational" market for its new model, offered with 2.5-litre four-cylinder and 4.7-litre V8 engines, but it didn't reckon on the likely demographic. More than 35,000 Scouts were sold in 1961 alone (instantly making the Scout the firm's best-selling product), with the 200,000th vehicle shifted in November 1968. Women figured highly among customers; the Scout proved more popular with female buyers than Jeep equivalents.

Maybe this sales success was boosted by models like the 1966 Scout 800 Sportop, with its neat hardtop and whitewall tires, and the "Red Carpet" limited edition, with its full carpeting. Or perhaps the success was due to the fact that there was nothing overtly militaristic about the car. Its straightforward styling suggests

healthy living just beyond suburbia, rather than combat overseas.

International was careful to maintain that aura when it revamped the vehicle as the Scout II in April 1971. Scout II's benign appearance was enlivened only by an upswept rear window line on the hardtop, while in 1973, when Scout sales hit 300,000, the vehicle adopted a Range Rover-like grille with bold vertical slats.

By now, International's success had been jealously noted by the Detroit giants. The Scout met well-marketed opposition from Ford, GM, and Jeep. Faced with vast investment costs to replace the car while endeavoring to keep pace with dramatically more stringent safety and emissions laws, International built the last Scout in 1980. Thus ended one of the last independent assaults on the established world order of the car industry, a venture that had led to two

important innovations. The first was that the Scout was the first off-road 4x4 vehicle to be offered with a turbocharger, but the second was more significant: International Harvester was the very first company to use the phrase "sport utility."

Despite International Harvester's ambitions for its Scout as a plaything for the outdoors life, shown right, many were in fact pressed into service, such as with the US police forces, opposite. The simplistic body design, below, makes the Scout a surprisingly ageless vehicle.

Jeep Wagoneer

With the Wagoneer, the SUV came of age at last. It's a tremendous example of thoroughly executed product design and, during its extraordinarily long life, it became such a fixture of America's roads that almost everyone seemed to overlook its groundbreaking significance.

The Wagoneer is, superficially, an uncompromisingly square-rigged, "two-box" van with a straight-edged glasshouse section jutting upward from a slablike main body pontoon. But such a description does it an injustice. Its lofty 5 ft. 3 in. (160 cm) height is masked not only by the waistline just below the window line but also by a full-length body crease and the ghosted outline of separate mudguards and running boards pressed into the lower side panels. Slim window pillars imbue the cabin with an airy, light-filled atmosphere.

At the front, an upright radiator grille on early models, looking rather like a church organ, did tend to emphasize the massiveness of the Wagoneer, but it was soon replaced by a full-width, horizontally slatted grille that gave the car an altogether sleeker look.

The Wagoneer's unveiling in 1962 was the centerpiece of an unprecedented product overhaul for Jeep. It was tagged "All new, and all-Jeep." Here, for the first time, was a vehicle developed from the ground up, rather than being ultimately derived from the venerable wartime hero. The company had skillfully blended the legendary Jeep go-anywhere ability and image with the classic station wagon in a package calculated—correctly—to appeal to the latent weekend outdoorsman in every American, while giving up little in the way of creature comforts. The Wagoneer, for instance, was the first off-roader to be offered with automatic transmission, and a potent V8 engine option was added in 1965 so the vehicle could

The earliest Wagoneer of 1962, below, shows off its perpendicular central radiator grille—just about the only thing that changed in three decades of continuous manufacture by Jeep, as proven by these 1980s examples shown opposite.

confront its bitter rival, the V8-powered International Scout. But unlike the Scout, the Wagoneer had four doors, another important innovation in the market. And, thanks to the attention to detail that stylist Brooks Stevens was allowed to lavish on the Wagoneer, the car had a newfound glamour. It looked, and continues to look, like a cool customer.

The Wagoneer's separate chassis also spanned pickup and panel van derivatives, called the Gladiator. Indeed, these massively outsold the Wagoneer at first. But that does not detract from the fact that the Wagoneer was genuinely the world's first purpose-designed SUV. It is also the longest-lived, by a country mile. Just six months after the Wagoneer was unveiled, the "Willys" name was ditched, and Jeep became a make in its own right. Despite frequent cosmetic makeovers—and some tacky trim

items such as fake wood paneling and white-wall tires—the Wagoneer continued largely unchanged until the end of the 1960s. It sailed on into the 1970s, with a two-door spin-off model carrying the Cherokee name for the first time in 1974; it soldiered through the 1980s too, finally finishing production in 1992 after three decades. The last examples were manifestly the same vehicles as the first ones, confirming the Wagoneer's status as a living classic in the same mold as the London taxi and the Citroën 2CV.

These pages show a galaxy of Wagoneer images taken throughout the vehicle's life. Designer Brooks Stevens certainly set out to change US motoring tastes with the car—the first SUV individually designed from the ground up—but he couldn't have known it would become a living legend.

Ford Bronco

Ford can be seen today as the first truly mainstream carmaker to enter the sport utility fray, in 1965, after earmarking the sector as one that had huge growth potential. The company also had a reputation by then for sometimes great flashes of design inspiration, particularly in sporty "personal" models like the Thunderbird, Mustang, and Cortina Lotus.

The 1965 Bronco, however, seems in retrospect an inauspicious start. Where the Jeep Wagoneer had some design finesse, the short-wheelbase Bronco was bluff, upright, and boxy. Ford's exterior design team had tried to transfer dartlike elements of the side profile of the Falcon sedan and Thunderbird coupé to the Bronco's sheer pressings in an attempt to cloak its straightforward derivation from Ford's pickup range, with which the Bronco shared steelwork forward of the windshield. But the top-hinged windshield wipers and a rubbing strip at the car's elevated waist level—something that looks as though it's there to ward off carelessly driven construction site hazards—give the game away. A radiator grille that looks like a cover for some industrial machine gas outlet doesn't help.

There were truck cab and full-length hardtop bodystyles, but the basic open-topped two-seater was the most innovative in offering a doorless design clearly intended to make the visual link in customers' minds between Ford pickup robustness and the carefree fun of the nascent beach-buggy scene. This version also turns the pressed-out horizontal section intended for that rubbing strip to stylistic advantage, the feature stooping down to cradle the door aperture before resuming its pugnacious process toward the Bronco's abruptly truncated tail. Ironically, however, this derivative wasn't very popular and was dropped after just three years.

The market for the Bronco was still known simply as the "off-highway" sector in the USA in 1965, when 50,000 corresponding vehicles were sold. Donald Frey, the Ford executive who had conceived and designed the Bronco in two years, saw this market rise to 70,000 by 1970, of which he wanted 25,000 to be Broncos. No doubt he was delighted at selling 18,200 in 1966, but it wasn't until 1973 that annual sales pierced the 25,000 barrier—before almost halving in the shadow of the fuel crisis.

Ford attempted to bolster the "sport" element of its first SUV, and confound its somewhat spartan reputation, by launching the special-edition Baja Bronco in 1970. Bill Stoppe and Parnelli Jones had made a name for the Bronco on the Baja 500 and 1000 off-road races in Mexico, and the car celebrated this achievement with hugely wide tires; flared rear fenders to accommodate them, however, had the effect of rendering this Bronco somewhat anonymous.

The Bronco had been a low-investment design for Ford, and by 1977 it showed: it was completely outshone by Chevrolet's Blazer in particular. In truth, the car should have been replaced three years previously, but the 1973 OPEC oil embargo spooked Ford into postponing it. Ford had the second-generation Bronco, codenamed Project Short Horn, ready to go in 1974, after product planners had

The versatile "fully doored" hardtop was the most popular choice among buyers of early Broncos. The beach buggy-like open version, opposite bottom, exuded adventurousness but proved to be something of a failure.

The compact Bronco II, above, was
launched in 1983. The original Bronco,
opposite top, could be configured as a
short-wheelbase pickup. A 2004 concept for
a new Bronco is shown opposite bottom.

insisted it must use the front end and doors of the 1973 F-100 pickup. From a design standpoint, this was an unpromising start for achieving a dynamic-looking end result, but a team headed by Dick Nesbitt came up with the ingenious idea of a wraparound roof band (with inspiration taken from the Porsche 911 Targa) for the hardtop. This meant that the pickup front structure could be used intact, the join between cab and rear compartment was concealed (instead of using a leak-prone thick rubber seal) because the hardtop overlapped it, and the Bronco gained a character that customers could mentally link directly to sports cars. The side window of the hardtop then curves round into the top panel, highlighting the Targa bar in side profile and making the Bronco look, for its considerable size, fairly sleek.

This innovative design was incredibly popular but destined to last only two years. The F Series gave it very tough legs, while the styling catapulted the Bronco past the market-leading Chevy Blazer (both were now known within the car industry as "full-size" SUVs, and the new Bronco was 2 ft./0.6 m longer than its predecessor). Yet Ford now wanted the Blazer to keep pace with its pickup program, and a new F Series in 1980 meant a new Bronco too.

The third-generation version was lighter, more economical, and cheaper to make. However, it was also a mildly altered doppel-ganger for the MkII. A restyle in 1987 nominally made the Bronco more aerodynamic, but from that point on it was preserved in design aspic. It wasn't inertia on Ford's part, more a shift of focus. The company had launched the Bronco II in 1983, helping establish the "midsize" of a rapidly formulating sector. The Bronco II is a more compact, neat-looking SUV based on the smaller Ranger pickup platform. It takes most of the Bronco's styling aspects and shrinks them around six-cylinder engines, with one of the principal differences being its more square-cut wheelarches when compared with the Bronco original. That car lived on to 1996, although the Bronco II lasted only until 1990.

Chevrolet/GMC Suburban

The Suburban name has been in constant use since 1936, making it (along with Morgan's Plus Four) the longest-lived model name in automotive history. General Motors would like us to believe that it's also the granddaddy of SUVs, but that isn't really the case. The early GMC Suburban was little more than a two-door panel van with windows and three rows of seats. It had two-wheel drive and fell very much into the commercial vehicle sphere, more likely to be bought by undertakers than large families. Year by year, as the basic GMC van design was updated, so was the Suburban, running through eras of high chrome, space-age detailing and then a shift to a spartan 1960s chic. It wasn't until 1957 that a four-wheel drive option was offered on the Chevrolet edition, edging the van furtively into Jeep territory. The addition of a third door on the passenger side inched the vehicle simultaneously into the realm of the car.

The real design breakthrough for the Suburban came for the 1973 model year, when a completely new style was revealed. "Only in America" is a phrase that could have been coined for what was now a truly elephantine station wagon. The style was, as before, closely allied to the Blazer and Chevrolet's pickups, which meant a huge, box-like nose and a straight-through fenderline. Starting just in front of the cavernous front wheelarches, a bulge rises vertically and then, turning at a 90° angle toward the top of the fender, continues as a prominent molding along the bodyside, giving the Suburban a towering, stepped look.

General Motors said the Suburban was more aerodynamic, although to modern eyes it would be difficult to tell quite how. It had four full doors, but in truth the vehicle was too large and trucklike to appeal to the actual suburbs. Its enormity, new full-time four-wheel drive, and stump-pulling V8 engine (a six was offered too) meant it was well suited to people living in remote areas where extreme weather conditions made a big difference to driving. It also found firm fans with public services such as fire and police departments, and sold well in the Middle East.

The first Suburbans, opposite, dated from 1936, and were simple, passenger-carrying conversions of GMC panel vans. This usable rationale continued in the 1940s and 50s, this page, as the basic van style evolved, and persisted under the Chevrolet badge.

Because of what the Suburban was and its unique place in the market at the axis of the car and truck world, its design evolution took place at an extremely conservative pace. Designers at GMC/Chevrolet only seemed to add to the impression of heavy metal by, for instance, replacing an already industrial-looking grille consisting of thirty-two chrome rectangles with an even blunter fifteen-rectangle one in 1977.

Further design changes included a sleeker nose in 1981, but it wasn't until 1992 that the Suburban was comprehensively updated. It now had a more generous glass area and a lower step-in height, but the proportion and the overall profile remained undiminished. Neither was the relationship changed with Chevrolet/ GMC trucks, on which Suburbans continue to be based wholesale. These vehicles are trucks first and foremost, and they continue as uncomplicated and distant, if long-lived, relations of the SUV as it has defined itself today. An all-new model launched in 2000 (when the GMC edition was renamed the Yukon) maintains that position.

The striking frontal treatment of the 1961 Suburban shown on this page featured the jukebox-like styling of contemporary Chevrolet and GMC pickups, while high ground clearance gave it excellent rough terrain capability.

Four-wheel drive came to the Suburban in 1957, bottom. The 1973 Suburban, right, has a massiveness that remains undiminished to this day, and has always offered more accommodation than most suburb-dwelling owners could ever need.

Mini Moke · Citroën Mehari · Renault Rodeo · Volkswagen 181

The pace of sport utility vehicle evolution during the 1950s and early 60s had been glacial, but it had also been overwhelmingly American, and North American at that. It seemed that only the USA offered the incubators of both massively challenging terrain and plentiful disposable income to put the pure sport, for which read "leisure," into utility.

Americans just got on with their lives after the Second World War, while Europeans had to rebuild theirs. Until the late 1950s most European cars were aimed at local economy motoring and "necessity" markets like taxis, police cars, and governmental use, or else they were tipped at the USA as exports. Any "fun" in European motoring, such as the 1959 Mini, tended to be accidental.

Two acts of motoring frivolity did finally emanate from Europe, however. And if these cars can't be said to mix "sport" with "utility," then few can. They were the Mini Moke and the Citroën Mehari.

The Moke—Australian slang for an obstinate pony—was the work of Alec Issigonis, the creator of the Mini itself. It's a solid, if misguided, example of lateral thinking in car design. The roominess of the compact Mini had been made possible by Issigonis's clever idea of transversely mounting the engine/gearbox with front-wheel drive to create a "powerpack." Why not install it in the automotive industry's "holy grail" product: a vehicle aimed at a lucrative military contract, much as the original Willys Jeep had been?

So Issigonis devised a military version shortly after he finished work on the ground-breaking sedan. A prototype was running by 1959, using a standard 850 cc Mini front-wheel drive engine/subframe in a simple, lightweight body—officially called a "buckboard"—that appeared to have been designed with Issigonis's set square. There was method in his compact, geometric madness, however: Mokes were intended to be stacked on top of each other, windshields folded flat and wheels resting on the mudguards of the car below, so they would be easy to pack into military transport aircraft. The Moke was meant to be parachuted into combat situations, and then be light enough to be carried on the shoulders of four burly soldiers if driving conditions overwhelmed it.

The stark outline of the Mini Moke was wholly practical. Its flat panels, and particularly its mudguards, were intended to make the car easy to stack in military transport planes, although no army ever employed the car in battle.

British Army chiefs put prototype Mokes on trial in 1960, but their low ground clearance, tiny 10-in. (254-mm) wheels, and two-wheel drive hindered progress over anything much more arduous than wet grass. True, the car could be hoicked across marshy ground, but any extra equipment, especially heavy weaponry, made carrying a Moke backbreaking work. The army decided to stick to Land Rovers.

Still, having splashed the cash developing the Moke, the British Motor Corporation (BMC) didn't want to waste it. So the vehicle went on sale in January 1964 as either an Austin or Morris Mini Moke and, with its open-sided canvas tilt/hood and storage lockers built into its sides, it was resolutely utilitarian, equipped with only a driver's seat and one windshield wiper. The only color option was dark green.

The target market was small businesses, one-man bands such as window cleaners, and delivery men, but in fact about 90% of Mokes

Citroën's Mehari, shown on this page, used its corrugated plastic body to best advantage as a genuinely rugged feature. Aimed at small businesses, it nonetheless had plenty of appeal as a "beach" car.

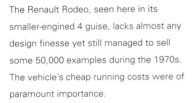

The Renault Rodeo, seen here in its smaller-engined 4 guise, lacks almost any design finesse yet still managed to sell some 50,000 examples during the 1970s. The vehicle's cheap running costs were of paramount importance.

paramount; it used the chassis and gas-sipping, air-cooled 600 cc engine from the Citroën Dyane. A four-wheel drive version was later offered, effective at tackling steep gradients, if painfully slow. But the Mehari's real innovation was in its thermoplastic bodywork, made from just eleven pieces, which because it was color-injected didn't need to be painted, thus removing a troublesome part of the car's assembly.

The corrugated bodysides and crude-looking frontal aspect performed two roles. First, they brought affinity with other famous Citroën vehicles, including the 2CV and the H-type van. Perhaps more importantly, the Mehari's lack of visual smoothness tended to deflect close attention from the quality of the plastic surface. The vehicle was available between 1968 and 1987, and 144,000 were sold.

Renault's Rodeo, while something of a "me-too" product, should not be overlooked since the company sold some 50,000 examples during the 1970s, as both the 4 Rodeo and 6 Rodeo. The Rodeo amounted to extremely basic plastic transport, developed for Renault as a quick response to the Mehari by a French van body builder called Teilhol. There is no design finesse to the Rodeo, although there is a rustic charm to its right-angled ugliness and features; it wears its easy-to-manufacture concept as a badge of honor. The Rodeo was just as likely as the Mehari to be found as a sand-filled holiday runabout, rather than cheap wheels for the self-employed French odd-job man.

And then there is the 181, Volkswagen's Beetle-based fun car with its corrugated body and fold-flat windshield. It was a rather stiff-looking and high-waisted affair, and its four doors were unusual. It was made from 1969 until 1979 mainly to satisfy a request for border control/field car transport for the German Army. This called for tight-lipped, military intent in the styling yet hardly the costly luxury of four-wheel drive. However, the army took just 16,000 of the 91,000 built. Most of the remainder of these charismatic, if pointless, machines were exported to the USA, where the model's American title hinted heavily at Volkswagen's own malaise about the model it had created: it sold the 181 there as "The Thing."

were exported and sold as hotel taxis in hot countries, or else lashed on to the back of large yachts for use in port. The Moke became a symbol of Mediterranean holiday fun, its role defined by its customers and not by its manufacturer, and although production ended in the UK in 1968, it lived on in Australia and then Portugal for another twenty-five years.

The Moke inspired no real rivals, but the Citroën Mehari fulfilled the same role of carefree open transport for sunny climates. Once more, it was conceived for one purpose and used for another. The Mehari was a four-seater pickup intended for a wide variety of industrial uses where operational economy was

This is the Volkswagen 181, also known as "The Thing" in the US market, conceived as transport for German border control troops at the height of the Cold War. Despite appearances, it had only two-wheel drive.

Savio Jungla · Fissore Scout · Moretti MidiMaxi

Italy's proud coachbuilding artisans were faced with a stark dilemma in the 1950s and 60s. It was a case of adapt or die. The country's uncommonly inspired designers and, more importantly, the craftsmen who translated this work into metallic reality were accustomed to basing their work on ready-made chassis frames provided by car manufacturers. Car-makers, likewise, considered themselves engineers, rarely making their own bodies. On these rolling foundations, a frame and panels could be built up by coachbuilders in any style a customer wanted.

Throughout the 1920s and 30s, this interdependent industrial relationship flourished. After the Second World War, technical advances meant that car structures shifted to "unitary" construction, in which the body and chassis were combined in one strong unit. Unpicking it to create individual designs was unfeasible.

Brave coachbuilding figures such as Battista "Pinin" Farina and Nuccio Bertone took the plunge and transformed their craft-based businesses into production-line factories, making large series of beautifully designed sporty niche models for Fiat, Alfa Romeo, and Lancia. But smaller, less well-financed concerns like Savio, Fissore, and Moretti—established in 1919, 1936, and 1945 respectively—were forced to look elsewhere for turnover-boosting activity. One area was in producing customized versions of Fiat's sedans, with either a luxury or a performance accent; and another was sport utility vehicles (although that's not how they were known at the time).

Savio was first with its Jungla in 1965. Its inspiration was probably a combination of the Mini Moke, the Willys Jeep, and the burgeoning Italian tourism industry with its beaches and resorts. The Jungla is a simple, open, four-seater

convertible, with little emphasis on workman-like practicality due to the fact that its rear-mounted Fiat 600 engine uses up any space that could otherwise have been devoted to freight. The half-hexagonal wheelarches, the flat windshield, the external hood catches—it's all a very long way from the smoothly curved Fiat 1100 coupé bodies that Savio had made in the 1930s. Still, needs must, and the Jungla was a hit, selling 3200 examples up to 1973; a later Jungla version of the 126 reduced the concept to its crude worst, and after 1989 Savio stuck to truck bodywork.

Fissore pulled off a similar trick with its Scout in 1971. Like the Jungla's, the steel chassis/plastic body combination was the coachbuilder's own, but every single mechanical part came from a regular Fiat production car, in this case the 127. Because the 127 grille and headlights are incorporated, the Scout

The Fissore Scout, above, may have lacked
sophisticated design but it fitted the bill
as a cheap and cheerful beach car.
Opposite is a similar Fiat 500-based
exercise from Moretti.

gives the impression of having a "real" car poking its head out of the front. The designer was Franco Maina, although what styling the Scout possesses is on the rough side of basic despite featuring the innovation of an enclosed, integral rollover bar—something that would feature strongly on SUVs in the future. Once again, the Scout sold surprisingly strongly (at one time 180 vehicles a month left Fissore's Turin plant), but the car died in 1982 along with the Fiat 127 itself.

Moretti, meanwhile, came up with its 127 Minijeep at exactly the same time, although it hastily re-branded it the MidiMaxi. There was also a 500-based model. It was an altogether more agricultural rendering of precisely the same idea. Doors are optional, and twin, parallel horizontal styling lines and tighter, straight-edged wheelarches give it a heavier, longer appearance.

None of these vehicles will ever merit a place at the car design top table; actually, they'd be lucky to be invited to the party. But they did jolt awake the demand in Europe for pure, nonperformance-oriented "leisure" vehicles. They were pioneers, then, of sorts, although not, as had been hoped, the saviors of Italian coachbuilding.

The Savio Jungla of 1965, opposite, was
the pioneer of the Fiat-powered "fun" cars
that attempted to sustain several of Italy's
old-established coachbuilders. The Moretti
MidiMaxi, above, cunningly incorporated
the hood and grille of the Fiat 127.

Range Rover

As a "tidying up" exercise, David Bache's inspired input into the Range Rover must rate as some of the finest weeks' work ever undertaken by a motor industry designer. It was a deftly executed and inspired showcase for his talents.

It must be said, however, that Bache had little to do with the Range Rover's concept—that of a comfortably sprung and powerful development of the Land Rover that would be as suited to driving on tarmac as it would be cutting its way across muddy farmland. Land Rover had considered a more civilized Land Rover/Rover car hybrid twice before. In the early 1950s it had toyed with a vehicle called "The Glasshouse," an ugly Land Rover-size station wagon with rear-wheel drive only; then, in the late 1950s, it had built prototypes of the Road Rover, a rather better-styled variation on the same theme. In both cases, the spur had been the profile of customers: a lot of them were rich, and their Land Rovers were often put to work on country estates, but another road car was usually required too.

The Range Rover came about as a result of several events. First, Rover engineers settled on coil springs to give the car a decent ride on roads, and then Rover management acquired the tooling for an excellent all-aluminum V8 engine from Buick. Putting these elements together in a Land Rover-type chassis, Rover engineers Spencer King and Gordon Bashford then created, almost instinctively, a "two-box" body shape for the car that also provided a split tailgate, with the bottom half dropping down and the top, glazed portion lifting up as an occasional hatchback. A horizontal styling line running right around the car neatly hid the shutline of the "clamshell"-type hood, while generously tall windows afforded a truly commanding view.

Other companies might have then given the Range Rover the green light for the showroom, even with its cheap-looking pressed steel nose resembling something from a delivery van, and its rather bland side profile. But Rover knew it had a great designer in Bache, who had produced the styling for the acclaimed P5 and P6 cars, and wisely allowed him to give the Range Rover the once-over.

Bache's approach was to make the vehicle a crisper design, with pronounced wheelarches rising from another horizontal styling line originating at the level of the chunky bumpers, raised edges to the hood, and a vertically slatted radiator grille pressing painted in matt black to disguise its cheapness and accentuate the circular headlamps that contrasted with the starched forms of the rest of the car. A very slightly indented section, about 1 ft. (30 cm) deep, is carried unwaveringly along the bodyside, between the two horizontal lines, to avoid slab-sidedness. Other details add to a surprising visual lightness for such a bulky vehicle, including door handles concealed in a vertical strip on the door edge, and the words "R-A-N-G-E R-O-V-E-R" in stick-on decals on the hood edge instead of a somber-looking Rover logo.

Bache also executed the interior, a necessarily simple affair, to tie in with the country set's desire for a car that could be hosed out after being crammed with Labradors but would still manage to look sleek and modern.

We perceive the Range Rover today to be a luxury car, but for its first ten years it was hardly plush inside. There was no power steering until 1973, no head restraints until 1979, and no auto-

matic gearbox until 1982. There wasn't even a four-door option until 1981, and even then it had been devised by a Swiss specialist called Peter Monteverdi, who subsequently received a royalty on every four-door Range Rover sold.

But the Range Rover did not date. It offered what was perceived to be an aristocratic alternative to American off-roaders from Jeep and Chevrolet, which meant it could be sold at a premium price. Its selection for exhibition at the Louvre in Paris in 1970 as an example of "modern sculpture" remains a unique endorsement, and it would be twenty-six years until the last of what became known as the Range Rover Classic was built.

A new Range Rover appeared in 1994. Presumably in an effort to demonstrate to customers, in what was now a vastly more competitive market, that they would be getting

The Range Rover is shown opposite in its original form and the 1980 "In Vogue" special edition. It is pictured on the right with its descendants, the four-door of 1981 and the 1994 MkII model, and vies for attention with a Land Rover, below.

more car for their money, the Range Rover gained a much-needed new interior. However, it was also a visually bulkier vehicle, with trademark details such as the round headlamps replaced by anonymous square ones, and Bache's artfully executed details trampled on in an effort to be somehow more contemporary. The reception was decidedly frosty. Temporary Land Rover custodian BMW wasted no time in replacing the car with an all-new Range Rover in 2001, taking the best of the King/Bashford/Bache original and twisting in some new character like twin ventilation louvres just in front of the doors to hint at the fiery V8 power inside, and double circular headlamps. For once, and despite an ownership transfer to Ford, a motoring design legend had been rescued in the nick of time.

The all-new Range Rover of 2001 saw a return to crisp lines and cute details, wrapped up in a package that is smooth-edged yet retains the brand's familiar image.

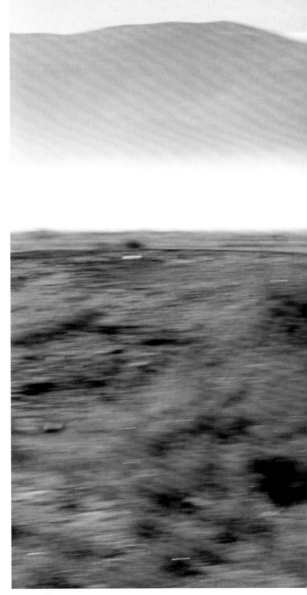

Suzuki Jimny · Daihatsu Taft · Daihatsu Terios

Until 1970, four-wheel drive off-roaders had tended to be large and powerful, reflecting either their battlefield roots or else the resources and spending power available to their target buyers. Yet, of course, it was only cumbersome vehicles that required high-capacity, thirsty engines. Moreover, a car designed primarily to pick its way along rutted tracks or through thick mud didn't always have to undertake its tasks in a hurry.

It was with all this in mind that Japan's Suzuki broached the SUV market with its LJ40 or Jimny (audaciously similar to the name on GMC's large 4x4 vehicles: Jimmy) in 1970, simultaneously creating a new design dynamic of "tall and small." Suzuki had graduated from being a pure motorcycle company to adding a line of Suzulight city cars in 1961, having been forced to examine overlooked market niches in its quest for expansion. The worldwide popularity of the Toyota Land Cruiser was a textbook success story in the emerging Japanese car industry, and Suzuki realized the potential in fusing its go-anywhere ability with small-car economy. And the engine really is small—a 360 cc two-cylinder affair offering a fraction of the Land Cruiser's power.

The LJ40's bodywork, however, is the twin of the contemporary Land Cruiser but two sizes smaller. Heavily ribbed bodysides and, on the hardtop version, a stepped level for the rear side window are distinctive, but even the word "SUZUKI" stamped into the grille panel apes the Toyota. All practical 4x4 vehicles need good ground clearance, and here the wheels are little smaller than the Land Cruiser's, exacerbating the Suzuki's narrow, upright stance.

The Daihatsu Taft, below, was a none-too-pretty attempt to prise open the center ground of the SUV market. Today's Suzuki Jimny, opposite, is the latest in a thirty-five-year-old dynasty and one of the world's smallest SUVs.

The vehicle's intended function was not so much to drive through featureless desert or tropical jungle but rather to provide practical light transport on mud track roads in developing countries such as Indonesia, hence the choice of hardtop, open, and pickup versions. In the mid-1970s, however, Australians began to take to the Jimny as a handy but tough runabout and then, with the launch of the four-cylinder 800 cc LJ80 model in 1978, it became a great success in both the French and British West Indies, where these tiny Suzukis rapidly became the standard-issue vacation rental car. The Jimny really did establish the lightweight 4x4 sector from scratch.

In 1982, a styling makeover removed any traces of Jeep/Land Cruiser-like detail, the new SJ410 models gaining uniformly round wheel-arches, boxy body proportions, and a grille with bold vertical slats in a miniature homage to the Range Rover. This car was, of course, perfect for town use because of its ultra-compact size, and was perhaps most responsible for the derision heaped on off-road vehicles that never actually saw any off-road action. The SJ was massively successful for Suzuki, however, and spawned a much more civilized, if even less credible looking, all-new Jimny in 1999, its styling an uncertain mixture of straight lines and curved profiles to the front fenders and grille.

Altogether harder to warm to, but still a significant vehicle, was the 1975 Daihatsu Taft, a direct response to the Suzuki Jimny phenomenon. The reason for the choice of the name of US president William Taft is a mystery; maybe it was Daihatsu's attempt to ingratiate itself with potential customers with its tall, narrow Jeep lookalike. In design terms the Taft has little of merit, its wheelbase appearing too short for its length; it was especially charmless, indeed, beside the perky little Suzuki. Its one innovative feature, on the open edition, is a built-in rollover bar linking the two B-posts with what looks like the giant "handle" of an outsize shopping basket.

Yet Daihatsu made a success of the Taft by, in 1976, uprating it from a 1-liter to a 1.6, later adding a diesel engine and a longer wheelbase option. In these guises, the Taft was an ideal, reasonably priced working vehicle for

The full spectrum of potential Jimny users was covered by Suzuki, below, with, in the early 1970s, the lion's share of attention focused on the rural sector rather than the hedonistic fun-seeker.

plugging across muddy industrial installations or towing farm equipment. In 1984 it was replaced by the fuller-figured but still resolutely cubic Rocky, which is still with us today.

Daihatsu made an arresting return to the micro-SUV market in 1997. It revealed the MS-X97, apparently a concept car but almost immediately on sale as the Terios. The company had done the math and correctly surmised that a five-door SUV like the Mitsubishi Pajero, traditional in everything except its large size, would be a strong seller, especially in Tokyo with its draconian parking taxes based on vehicle length. The Terios, therefore, courted ridicule by offering the package on a miniature scale, but it has been quite successful for people who can rationalize that they will only use the vehicle in an urban environment but cannot resist the marketing pull of four-wheel drive and aura of the SUV. If nothing else, the Terios helps automotive biodiversity, and is a plausible, high-riding alternative to a supermini. There have been no imitators, however.

The original Suzuki Jimny, above, cleverly repackaged the qualities of the Toyota Land Cruiser for a different group of buyers more concerned with low running costs than outright performance. The Daihatsu Terios, left, almost certainly the world's smallest four-door SUV, is aimed at city dwellers.

Chevrolet Blazer

The Blazer was something of a design-it-yourself machine. At the one extreme, it was possible to specify it literally as transport for solitary enjoyment of the great outdoors. That would have meant a totally open-topped vehicle with just a single seat for the driver. It's a description you could also apply to a Formula 1 racing car but, of course, the two couldn't be further apart.

Whereas the Suburban had grown out of a Chevrolet delivery van, the Blazer was spawned directly by Chevrolet's long-running pickup series, a bolted-together vehicle line forming the backbone of working America. By 1969, when the Blazer made its debut, the Suburban was also a member of the same pickup-based band, but where the Suburban put the accent on carting personnel to hostile outposts, the Blazer was aimed, nominally, at the weekend sportsman who might, indeed, want to wander off on his own with enough space to haul back a dead moose or two. Of course, almost all Blazer buyers wanted more versatility than that and so went for a passenger seat, a bench seat in the

rear, and the optional glassfiber hardtop to create a roomy and rugged station wagon.

The design basics of the Blazer (the GMC Jimmy, incidentally, was identical) were shared with the pickups and the Suburban: a routinely square "box" for the engine and another for the cabin. The fundamental change occurred in 1973, when the entire series received a sculpted bodyside and curved side glass, while round wheelarches gave way to aggressively cut square ones. The whole design dynamic was changed from the bland acceptability of straight horizontal lines and round shapes for wheelarches and headlamps to uncompromisingly brutal features and a bulkier waistline. On the Blazer, this neo-American look has endured untrammeled by automotive fashions to the present day. About as close to evolution as Chevrolet's stylists seem to have come is to have gradually filed off some of the vehicle's sharper edges as a nod to contemporary trends. Still, the massiveness of the rectangular grille, the bluff passenger compartment, and the

bumper/side-molding to lower bodywork volume ratio was essentially unaltered.

In 1995, the Blazer name was replaced by Tahoe, although there was no change in styling philosophy. The change was more to allow market differentiation between this now "full-size" off-roader and a smaller Blazer, the S-10. A sort of "regular/midsize" iteration of the original, it shared its underpinnings with Chevrolet's smaller S-10 pickup line. Seen side by side, the size difference between the two Blazers is marked, but the S-10 broadcasts its more compact character with single headlamps in place of two stacked on top of each other. Engines were notably less muscly too, starting with a 2-liter four-cylinder unit and only going

The images on these pages show, clockwise from opposite top, the blunt contours of a 1977 Blazer; two-tone paint in the Exterior Decor package, of a similar vintage; the sculpted look, which arrived in 1973; the more compact S-10 Blazer; and the toned-down machismo of a 1992 model.

Chevrolet Blazer

up to a 2.8 V6—no prairie-wild V8 power here. It was a retreat to the size of SUV exemplified by Ford's original Bronco. When the Bronco and the first Blazer had been concurrent in 1969, the Blazer was an incredible 1 ft. (30 cm) wider and 2 ft. (60 cm) longer than the Bronco. Now both Chevrolet and Ford (with the Bronco II in 1983) were returning to fill this gap, presumably having gotten wind of Jeep's impending Cherokee. Next to Jeep's thoughtfully executed product, the S-10 is a crude piece of product cross-breeding, but the marketing juggernaut of Chevrolet (there was a GMC Jimmy S-15 doppelganger too) could only ensure it was a success with buyers who considered a full-size Blazer to be just that little bit too hardcore.

This page shows three views of the earliest Blazers, which featured semicircular wheelarches. Below is an example of the unusual high-riding convertible model; despite the outdoors image, it wasn't a particularly popular option.

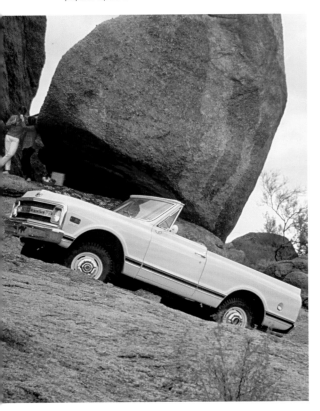

The Blazer, as seen in 1973 and 1974, had square-cut wheelarches that gave a much more aggressive, rugged image. This car was to prove immensely popular, opening up the large SUV market for General Motors and Jeep to exploit later.

Subaru Leone

If you look carefully, this book is full of caveats and exceptions. Such is the tangled nature of the SUV's genesis. The Subaru Leone, for instance, cannot be regarded as an SUV in the usual idiom. It is a station wagon and, ostensibly, a perfectly ordinary one.

Yet under the Leone's rather dull lines, its unique selling point makes it a true milestone in car design. It was the first conventional family car with a four-wheel drive system. Not the first four-wheel drive road car; that was the Jensen FF luxury coupé that entered the market seven years before the Leone went on sale in 1973. The Jensen, however, was a specialist car,

impractical for four adults and with a price tag that put it into the supercar league. It was the Leone that first planted the idea of four-wheel drive as an everyday driving advantage in the minds of "ordinary" motorists.

The Leone's styling was shared with other versions of the vehicle, introduced in 1971 and a steady development of the 1967 FF1 family car with its flat four-cylinder engine and front-wheel drive. The overall profile is a forward-leaning one, with a long frontal overhang and a curtailed rump, and a waistline that originates at the corner of the front fender, dips down at the rear passenger door, and then rises up and

The Subaru Leone 1600 4WD estate, shown below and opposite top, has unremarkable styling that belies its significance as the world's first popular four-wheel drive family car. The pickup version, opposite bottom, was much admired by farmers.

over the rear wheelarch—the proportions of the ubiquitous "Coke bottle" line adopted in the late 1960s and early 1970s, of which the Ford Cortina MkIII and the American Motors Javelin were spectacular examples.

Details on the Leone—insignia, light surrounds, and vents—were overstyled for the time, coating the compressed Detroit proportions with fussy oriental ornamentation, but the car at least looks eager in an awkward sort of way. Riding slightly higher than an average sedan, the Leone only hints at its off-road capability through its more knobbly tires, its "4WD" emblems, and the standard mudflaps that sit behind each wheel.

The Leone was launched gradually in export markets, and it started to forge a great reputation for Subaru. Initially the car was aimed at the farming community, and was usually marketed in tandem with a Leone-based pickup that was also likely to have great rural appeal. As the Subaru brand evolved, however, its appeal was widened. The pickup carried the impudent sobriquet "Brat" in the USA to boost its credibility among American truck devotees, and Subaru made significant inroads into premium Alpine markets such as Switzerland and Austria, where its four-wheel drive really was a practical asset in icy, mountainous areas.

Later models mustered a choice of bodystyles including a three-door hatchback, while in 1981 a turbocharged 1800 cc engine option began to propel Subaru along its chosen furrow toward being the purveyor of extremely capable four-wheel drive sports sedans exemplified by the rally-winning Impreza. Only much later did the company belatedly apply its strengths to the SUV proper with the Forester (see p. 176), having oddly failed to capitalize on the early lead the outwardly conventional Leone had given it.

From most views, the original Leone, right and opposite, is an awkward-looking car with fussy detailing, but Subaru finally hit the "good styling" trail in 1981 when it launched a remarkably coupé-like second-generation pickup, top, sometimes sold as the Subaru Brat.

Monteverdi Safari - Lamborghini LM

Conspicuous Arabic consumption, thanks to the vast profits of OPEC in the gas-hungry days of the mid-1970s, was something the luxury goods industries of "Old Europe" pursued with unbridled gusto. Whether it was fashion, furniture, property, or gadgets, the spending power of the extended ruling classes in Qatar, Saudi Arabia, Oman, Kuwait, and the United Arab Emirates was ruthlessly courted in London, Paris, Geneva, and Milan. And if money-no-object desert drivers wanted extraordinary cars custom-made for their own lifestyles, then that was what they had to have.

The Jeep Wagoneer and Range Rover had been the first vehicles to provide opulence with a four-wheel drive ability used in shifting sand rather than squelching mud. However, these were regular production-line offerings to a standard specification. Middle Eastern one-upmanship had to be catered to by various small conversion specialists, and the design of such vehicles, which were bound for some of the least regulated car markets on earth, varied enormously in quality.

The Swiss GT carmaker Peter Monteverdi was really the first to cater specifically to the faddy tastes of motoring sheikhs. Monteverdi had proved himself adept as a car industry magpie, designing his cars around existing components and contracting production out to Italian coachbuilders, and the Monteverdi Safari of 1976 was no exception. It used the running gear of the International Scout, although it also featured an optional Chrysler V8 engine, and only the truly eagle-eyed would have detected the Scout's doors and windshield as a hint to the all-American structure beneath. To this, however, was grafted a carlike nose, with Monteverdi's trademark four-headlamp grille, and a neatly proportioned Range Rover-like rear that actually incorporates an entire Range Rover tailgate assembly. A decadently trimmed interior completes the package, and, in general, the vehicle presents quite a chic, well-tailored image.

When the car was revealed at the Geneva Motor Show in 1976, Middle Eastern buyers

lapped up the vehicles at Monteverdi's extortionate prices, and he soon added the Sahara, simply a standard Scout with a Monteverdi grille and a better interior. The termination of Scout manufacture in 1980 put an end to these vehicles (although the King of Morocco is said still to drive his Safari), but it did not quell the appetite for something similar. This appetite was satisfied from the most unlikely of quarters: Lamborghini.

During one of the Italian supercar manufacturer's most financially rocky periods, it teamed up with California's Mobility Technology International to devise a brand new light military vehicle that would impress the US Army into giving the consortium a lucrative contract. The result was the Lamborghini

The Monteverdi Safari, opposite, hid its prosaic American origins thanks to a clever Swiss–Italian makeover. The Lamborghini LM002, above, presented an irresistible attraction to fickle Middle Easterners, particularly because it had this useful outside space, left, on which to transport the retinue.

Cheetah, unveiled at the Geneva Motor Show in 1977, and a total shock to those people used to the sensual shape of Lamborghini supercars.

The sand-colored Cheetah took the form of a giant, high-riding dune buggy, a five-seater with no doors to its indestructible-looking passenger "cage" and balloon-like tires affording massive ground clearance. The rear end was dominated by the most practical of features: two jerrycans, an ax, and a towing eye that made the Cheetah look like it could easily haul a broken-down tank. The vehicle's similarity to the 1991 Hummer H1 is uncanny, if not downright suspicious.

Cheetah prototypes with Chrysler V8 engines were apparently tested to, literally, destruction in the USA, while a loan from the Italian government partly funded the vehicle, soon rechristened LM001 (for Lamborghini Military). For whatever reason, an order never materialized, and that might well have been that. Then someone at Lamborghini remembered all that Arab cash and those inhospitable, yet prestige-hungry, Middle Eastern roads.

The LM002 was announced at the Monaco Grand Prix in 1982. It was the Cheetah tamed into an extraordinary four-door sedan with jagged, ruler-straight lines and a rudimentary if macho-looking hood extension to house Lamborghini's all-aluminum 5.2-liter V12 engine. An LM004 version could be ordered with an even more powerful marine V12 at 7.2 liters, making this the only SUV with a V12 engine and the biggest capacity by far. At the back, an open-topped load area, accessed through a drop-down tailgate, could carry six more passengers.

By fall 1985 the LM002 was actually on sale, and orders came flooding in from the Middle East. It was still available in 1993, but the arrival of the Hummer—even tougher but with none of the temperamental troubles of a hand-built Italian vehicle with a supercar-derived V12 powerplant—scuttled any remaining interest. The LM002 was the only true SUV supercar until Porsche's Cayenne, and something of a mythical beast (it could do almost 100 mph/160 kph across sand) to schoolboys and military fantasists worldwide.

The design groundwork laid by Lamborghini's Cheetah wasn't wasted; the car inspired the audacious Lamborghini LM002, which is about as close as the SUV has come to becoming a supercar. It remains the only production off-roader to have featured a V12 engine.

Volkswagen Iltis · Mercedes-Benz G-Wagen

With an ignoble military heritage, the German motor industry was a hesitant newcomer to off-roaders, and the late 1970s were to see two contrasting attempts to test the water—one that would prove astonishingly short-lived, the other a paragon of design continuity.

The Volkswagen Iltis undoubtedly had some ingenious features that, to a military operator, would have been very handy. A four-wheel drive system in which the front wheels only could be used for road driving would have saved fuel, while suspension components interchangeable between front and rear would have cut down on repair times and inventories.

These were just some of the virtues of the Iltis, launched in 1978. It was a development of the light, four-wheel drive field car called the Munga that had long been made by DKW, one of Audi's former associate companies under the Auto Union umbrella organization. The Iltis was created in response to an order for 8800 vehicles from the German Army at a time when it was inconceivable to offer the contract to foreign tender if there was a German company that could fulfill the task: a Land Rover would have done just fine, but a German alternative was infinitely preferable. And, although engineered by Audi, the Iltis gained a Volkswagen emblem in line with VW's status as a beacon of German postwar industrial endeavor.

However, the Iltis looked almost amphibious, with its reptilian, tapering nose, short wheelbase, and ribbed sides. The "roof" was little more than a flimsy plastic tilt. With military deliveries proceeding smoothly, Volkswagen decided to offer it to the public too in a "leisure" iteration, although this version was barely more comfortable than the basic army model, and expensive at DM 35,225 in 1980.

The Iltis found it impossible to disguise its military heritage, top right, and proved a poor seller in the civilian market. Introduced in 1979, the G-Wagen, right and opposite, has since become a "living legend."

Times had changed, however: when civilian Iltis production stopped three years later, only 747 of the vehicles had been built, and it took an incredible four more years to sell them all. Consumers were simply unwilling to have a military spin-off foisted on them any longer; the ugly, basic, yet undoubtedly capable Iltis might have been lapped up in the 1950s, but not the 1980s.

In stark contrast, Mercedes-Benz's Geländewagen was launched in 1979 and is still in robust health twenty-five years on. Even M-B calls it a "living legend," a lovely motor industry

The two-door convertible G-Wagen, left and below, was added to the range in 1996 in an effort to give this indomitable vehicle a more youthful image.

metaphor for any ancient model that still sells without any extra investment needed to sustain it.

The G-Wagen's secret, if there is one, is easy to see. The vehicle cut a middle path between the brazen utility of a Land Rover and the snob appeal, together with the modern, comfortable coil-spring suspension, of the Range Rover, while offering Mercedes-Benz standards of cabin ergonomics and fastidious build quality. Where the trail-blazing British products had been rushed into production with plenty of compromises, Mercedes took its time to get the vehicle just right, and even enlisted a joint-venture partner, Austria's Steyr-Daimler-Puch, to oversee the entire development and then manufacture the G-Wagen at its plant in Graz. Accordingly, the G-Wagen took eight years to

bring to market, and has a typically German aesthetic for the time of heavy-looking forms combined with obvious visual toughness; the slab-fronted black plastic grille panel, for instance, is eminently practical. The fact that the partners elected for angular forms that exuded utter practicality—the antithesis to "styling" as such—hints at the caution behind the venture; nine years after the Range Rover had broken out as a 4x4 image car, Mercedes still hedged its bets on a vehicle look that would appear seemly in local authority service.

The decision was made from the outset to offer the G-Wagen in various versions, using a hand-built body-on-chassis manufacturing approach that would always make it an expensive vehicle. However, this approach made it possible for each customer to conceive

and order a G-Wagen in exactly the way he or she wanted it (short- or long-wheelbase, gas or diesel engine, open or closed bodywork), while still—crucially—getting a Mercedes-Benz at the end of the process.

For wealthy Middle Europe landowners there is nothing like a G-Wagen, and a constancy of orders makes the vehicle a never-changing cornerstone of SDP's output. The emergence of the Hummer H1 as a consumer product has given the G-Wagen, now also referred to as the G-Class, a late-life fillip. The G-Wagen's debut in the USA in 2001, complete with a five-door station-wagon body, 5-liter V8 engine, and sumptuous interior, gave status-conscious buyers (mostly coastal ones, perhaps) just what they were looking for—a "Hummer" with class.

How long the G-Wagen's popularity can continue is open to question. "Indefinitely" would be one answer, since to change and modernize its design radically might mean an enormous investment, and would also kill its engineering-led, custom attraction that keeps some 6000 buyers coming back for more each year; the cumulative total is now over 175,000. As DaimlerChrysler chief Jürgen Hubbert has said: "Even after a quarter of a century, the G-Class still has plenty of potential. This cross-country classic continues to set the standards in its market segment." To that end, a new G55 AMG model offers a supercharged 476 bhp V8 engine from the renowned German tuning firm in its title. It can hit 62 mph (100 kph) in 5.6 seconds and has 700 Nm (516 lb./ft.) of torque, which is blistering stuff for a near thirty-year-old design. In its unchanging looks, Mercedes likes to compare its G-Wagen to other long-lived cars, including the Land Rover and the Morgan sports car, as well as the Burberry raincoat, the Mont Blanc "Meisterstück" fountain pen, and the Jaeger-LeCoultre Reverso watch. Self-flattery, maybe, but there's no denying the G-Wagen its classic status.

The ultra-boxy five-door G-Wagen is shown in its ultimate form with a 5-liter AMG-tuned engine. It was this model that belatedly took the G-Wagen to the USA in 2001, twenty-two years after its launch.

Matra Rancho

The impact of the Rancho is lost on us almost three decades since its debut in 1977, but its importance to the design story of the SUV is seismic.

The Rancho is not, however, an "off-road" car. It cannot perform the farm duties of a Land Rover nor power across desert like a Toyota Land Cruiser. Indeed, it doesn't actually have four-wheel drive, making it another one of those conundrums that have popped up in the SUV story so far. None of these things matters.

What the Matra amply demonstrated was that there was a large appetite among buyers for a roomy and highly practical vehicle that complemented an active lifestyle but didn't have the complexity (nor, indeed, the heavier fuel consumption and associated running costs) of four-wheel drive. Moreover, the Rancho was a highly cost-effective design; it took very little to put into production and, for a car that could be sold at a premium price because of its novelty, component prices were below average. There was no loser here.

The Rancho was the work of Antoine Volanis, a designer employed by the aerospace-to-sports car company Matra whose talents had already been demonstrated on the Matra Bagheera sports car. The Bagheera used a Simca engine and was sold through Chrysler Europe's Simca dealer network, so these conduits were already established for the Rancho. In effect, the Rancho is a rebodied Simca 1100 pickup: all the metalwork from the nose to the two passenger doors, and including the cabin roof, was maintained. Then a steel-framed, glassfiber passenger section was attached at the back, its lightness meaning that the rear overhang could be extended far beyond the truncated end of the standard pickup.

The rear "van" area has a much higher roofline, giving a stepped profile, even after a glassfiber cargo tray with a steel retaining rail was added to the Simca's roof to hide cleverly the join between front and rear sections. All the standard Simca glass is retained at the front, but the rear has huge side windows, the upper section making it one of the airiest cars available, while the lower part is divided and can be slid open. A split rear tailgate apes the

Rarely encountered today, Matra's Simca-based Rancho whetted the European public's appetite for cars with an "off-road" image for outdoor lifestyles. Note the swiveling spotlights mounted at the base of the windshield, maybe taking the safari theme to implausible extremes.

Range Rover in having a lift-up glass upper section and a drop-down plastic lower one.

Black plastic cladding to side rubbing panels and wheelarch surrounds gives the Rancho a chunkiness the Simca never had, while a matching black plastic front bumper, with large spotlamps covered by purposeful-looking grilles in semicircular recesses, together with a bluff steel "bullbar," hides the car's prosaic underpinnings even further. Hand-adjustable spotlights mounted on the scuttle just in front of the windshield maybe take the safari theme a bit too far, or perhaps they are just a touch of Gallic design humor.

The Rancho has been taunted ever since its launch by pundits for being all-show and no-go, a pretentious car with front-wheel drive that could never deliver what its manly exterior promised. This is despite later versions that offered a seven-seater option and also a "Découvrable" model, with roll-up canvas sides, that really could have been a mobile vantage point from which to watch wildlife.

However, the Rancho was a success with buyers, with 56,457 vehicles being sold between 1977 and 1983, and its low investment (flat glass

and plastic never did come very expensive) made it an ingeniously profitable venture for all concerned. Its demise was concurrent with that of the underlying Simca itself, for which there was no pickup replacement. More importantly, from a design standpoint, the Rancho confirmed

that "image" would now be vital to any successful small SUV; just as there were little-trumpeted two-wheel drive options to many US off-roaders, the Rancho had proved that this feature was of secondary importance to the "lifestyle" market it had opened up.

The "Chrysler" legend on the number plate, opposite top, signifies the Rancho's inception at the tail end of the US firm's European venture, just as the division was sold to Peugeot in 1978. Later versions, opposite bottom, boasted a seven-seater option thanks to two extra, rear-facing seats. You'd hardly think it was a Simca van under all that plastic cladding, right.

Nissan Patrol/Terrano

The hard points in Nissan's SUV design story are well spaced out, but for fifty years they have centered on the Patrol. If you know this vehicle then you will recognize it as an extremely capable off-road machine, large and rugged, invariably equipped with a diesel engine of phenomenal durability. If you don't, then you will still have seen Patrols in the white fleet of the United Nations, hard at work in the background of news bulletins, in some of the world's most war-torn corners. The Patrol is less well-known than the Toyota Land Cruiser, but just as dependable.

Japanese car companies gained a reputation in their early days—by which is meant anything much before 1960—for mimicking Western products. The early Patrol is a prime culprit. Introduced in 1951, it is an unremarkable "interpretation" of the Willys Jeep/Toyota Land Cruiser genre, faithful even down to the similar positions of the grab handles and the grille-to-headlights ratio. There was no interest in either the defense or the leisure markets; the Patrol was aimed at police and fire services and could be supplied in all sorts of specific guises. By 1959, an all-steel eight-seater station wagon still looked little different from the Willys version of a decade earlier. During this reconstructive period in Japan, Nissan was primarily a truck-maker anyway, but, as the company embraced the car market proper in the 1960s and 70s, the Patrol remained a Cinderella product, exported only to developing nations such as India—unchanging, but a steady seller.

Doubtless influenced by the success of the Range Rover, the Patrol was hauled up to date by 1980, gaining modern, fully enclosed bodywork for the first time in both short-wheelbase three-door and long-wheelbase wagon guises. As for styling, there was none to speak of; the Patrol's arch lines are razor-sharp and towering in proportion, a high waist and a relatively shallow glasshouse contributing to a slightly hunched and ill-proportioned stance in the three-door, where the car looks too long for its wheelbase. A fixed rear seat in the wagon severely hampers versatility, although there is still massive cargo room inside.

In this form, the Patrol saw limited exports, but nonetheless began to gain considerable respect for its capabilities. For eight years its design stagnated, but a clever makeover in 1987 to produce the Patrol GR used heavily flared fenders at the front and back to house wider wheels, while an additional grille molding added curvature to the vehicle's sheer frontage. In retrospect, it was a remarkably effective facelift that kept the Patrol in the running until it was replaced by an entirely new model in 1997. Sizewise, this version is the same giant, but its contours are smoother and neater, if a little anonymous by the rapidly evolving standards of the twenty-first century.

Unprepossessing but extremely tough, the 1980 Patrol, opposite, was the first to be marketed internationally by Nissan. Today's Patrol, above and right, is one of the largest SUVs available, and also one of the least adventurous in styling terms.

The Patrol was the wrong vehicle to spearhead an assault on the SUV market in the United States. The Terrano turned out to be the right one. Nissan took a leaf out of the Ford/Chevrolet book of cunning by converting its four-wheel drive pickup into a distinctive-looking three-door off-roader in 1986. The Terrano cut an interesting figure with its asymmetrically split rear side windows, a diagonal, forward-leaning pillar forming one rhombic- and one triangular-shaped pane of glass. The effect was to put a suggestion of forward movement into what was, essentially, quite a slab-sided vehicle.

The Terrano gained the Pathfinder tag in the US market, where it proved a popular hit, with a rather dull-looking five-door model joining it in 1989. Forcing its way through consumer resistance to a Japanese inroad in the traditional US-dominated SUV market, the Pathfinder laid the foundations for Nissan's present-day SUV winner, the X-Trail.

In side profile, the latest Patrol, opposite top, stays true to the voluminous dimensions of previous models, such as the GR, left, launched in 1987. The car looks too long for its wheelbase in this short-wheelbase early 1980s Patrol, opposite bottom. The 1986 Terrano/ Pathfinder, below, was based on Nissan's four-wheel drive pickups.

Mitsubishi Pajero

Nineteen eighty-two was the year when the SUV finally matured into a truly consumer-friendly product thanks to Mitsubishi's Pajero (Montero in Spanish-speaking territories and the USA, and Shogun in the UK). Instantly and widely imitated by catch-up competitors, it was a ground-up design, with no throwbacks to previous vehicles and no carryover components to render the driving experience a tank- or truck-like one.

Interestingly, Mitsubishi Motors already had decades of experience building four-wheel drive vehicles. In 1953 it had obtained the exclusive license to produce the Willys Jeep Universal in Japan and, amazingly, it was still

doing so in 1998 some eleven years after the Universal/CJ had finally been retired in the USA. It made 205,000 of them. The Universal was always a commercial vehicle, and intimate knowledge of the trusty Jeep no doubt convinced Mitsubishi that it was definitely not the basis of a successful assault on the SUV market.

Instead, Mitsubishi formulated the Pajero on a human scale, jettisoning the battlefield aura of the Jeep and almost scaling up the "two-box" shape of the typical supermini. The first Pajero came as a three-door wagon that, while still a large car, was not threateningly so. The hoodline is low and the cabin tall, making entry and exit through generously wide doors far

easier than the "mounting" needed on, for example, truck-based SUVs from the USA. There is plenty of tumblehome to the bodyside: subtly curved door glass, with the metalwork tapering in between the wheels, helps reduce the visual bulk endemic to big off-roaders. A horizontal styling line takes in the wheelarch shapes and links them to a slightly protruding sill, once again anchoring the car to the road in the view of the observer. A thoughtfully designed interior makes the most of the copious quantities of light streaming in through the big windows.

It wasn't just the surfaces of the Pajero that were excellently resolved. The front torsion bar

The first Pajero is shown opposite; an early convertible model is pictured left. Early design sketches, below, sought to distance the car from Mitsubishi's Jeep-making background. The MkII Pajero, bottom, proves itself in off-road rallying.

suspension allied to traditional leaf springs at the back presented an astonishingly good on-tarmac ride, while the Pajero was the first ever turbodiesel passenger car to emerge from Japan, and an excellent performer to boot. Even Mitsubishi was amazed when a near-standard Pajero scored a legendary victory in the production car class in the Paris–Dakar desert race in 1982, on its maiden attempt.

The Pajero was certainly a pacesetter with its easy-to-live-with style, comfort, and performance; today, after two total redesigns (the first, in 1991, rounded off the styling even further; the second, in 1999, endowed the car with more flourish in an increasingly crowded sector), it has earned itself a firm place among the large SUV establishment.

The early Pajero three-door, opposite top,
was designed to be easy to access,
own, and drive. The MkI Pajero five-door,
opposite bottom, shows the raised
roof section for increased passenger
headroom. Three- and five-door variants
of the 1991–2001 era MkII Pajero, shown
on this page, had a well-deserved
reputation for reliability and quality.

Isuzu Trooper/Amigo

Japan's Isuzu joined the SUV fray in a big way in 1989 with its MU, an acronym for the charmingly entitled "Mysterious Utility." Through manufacture on three continents, it would become an unlikely world product—unlikely because, in fact, it was not terribly sophisticated in either its design or its engineering.

Isuzu used its existing four-wheel drive pickup chassis, a ladder-frame affair, as the car's basis, along with the pickup's metalwork from the grille to the windshield. From there back, there was the choice of a slope-backed five-door wagon or a two-door with either a hardtop over the rear seats or a canvas hood. With either of these covers removed, the appearance was pseudo-sporty; in the hood-down position the Isuzu adopted the flat-decked look of a sports car in the Porsche 911 Targa/Lancia Beta Spider mold. Both of those "role models" were

The Trooper, launched in 1981, is shown opposite bottom in its original form. Subsequent models, arrayed around it, have deviated little from the design aesthetic established at the outset.

relatively ancient by 1989, and the Isuzu likewise looked dated and clumsy, the thickness of its roof pillars—especially the hugely long B-pillar on the two-door—portraying a bloated look, or a solid one, depending on your viewpoint. Nonetheless, the blistered wheelarches certainly look good wrapped around large, fat wheels and tires, and the spare wheel hanging out the back suggests ruggedness at the same time as boosting interior cargo space.

Mysterious Utility was built in Japan, in Indiana, USA, and in Bedfordshire in the UK, and it was variously sold as the MU, the Isuzu Amigo, the Isuzu Rodeo, the Vauxhall Frontera, the Opel Frontera, and even the Honda Passport. Astute pricing meant it brought many more

customers to the budget-price, small-size SUV market. It definitely offered better passenger (for which, read: family) accommodation than anything from Suzuki at the time. Isuzu's hope must have been that many owners would eventually trade up to an Isuzu Trooper, a larger SUV that entered the market in 1981, a redoubtably capable four-wheel drive workhorse with flat contours and a lofty stance. Throughout the 1980s and 90s, the Trooper typically came as a vanlike three- or five-door vehicle with a tough and powerful 3–3.5-liter diesel engine. Stylistically unassuming, and

with a certain appeal because of that, the Trooper was bought by farmers and coastguardsmen and a coterie of private buyers who needed something gutsy to tow a horsebox.

Yet not even the Trooper was Isuzu's first stab at an SUV. That honor goes to the 1967 Unicab, an open-topped field car-type machine that used the entire mechanical drivetrain from the Isuzu Bellet sedan—meaning, of course, that it was just a two-wheel drive (the rear ones) vehicle. The Unicab looks like it might be fun to trundle around in on a blazing hot afternoon, but on a cold, gray day it would resemble little

more than a pile of suitcases on a four-wheeled trolley, with its headlamps set rather too close together for comfort. Quite what buyers did with their Unicabs is uncertain; this is the true "mysterious utility" in Isuzu's checkered past.

A rare photo of a rare vehicle, the Isuzu Unicab, launched in 1967, is shown below. Despite its robust appearance, it lacked four-wheel drive. The opposite page features examples of the Opel Frontera, one of the many guises of that "Mysterious Utility," the Isuzu Amigo.

Lada Niva

With their hundreds of square miles of inhospitable terrain, criss-crossed by roads that are little more than tracks, Russia and its satellite territories would seem a fertile breeding ground for four-wheel drive vehicles. Besides, more than fifteen years since the dawn of the perestroika era, one would expect an environment where a little bit of "sport" might now be mingling with the requirement for sheer "utility."

In fact, there has only been one Russian vehicle that has come close to the SUV concept. It is, however, quite a remarkable one. It is the VAZ 2121, more often known by the title of Lada Niva, and it was unveiled in 1977. The Niva was the company's first totally independent design, since all the cars it had built up to that point had been based on the Fiat 124.

Westerners might be forgiven for thinking the Niva (which means crop or field) was made obsolete many years ago; it was a regular fixture of price lists in Europe (although never the USA) throughout the 1980s, but had largely vanished by the mid-1990s because a lack of investment to update it meant the vehicle fell foul of more stringent safety and emissions legislation. Yet, in fact, it continues to be a strong, profitable seller for AutoVaz despite its 1977 design being seemingly frozen in time. It's a classic, almost.

It is a testimony to the Niva's design excellence that it has lasted so long. Its straightforward boxiness is offset by well-proportioned, semicircular wheelarches linked by a swage line in the metalwork. Prominent bumpers at the front and rear clearly mean

business, while the Niva's most distinctive feature is its hood, which opens by taking the upper edges of the front fenders along with it for wide-open engine access. Sandwiched between the top of the rectangular grille and the hood, oblong indicator lights occupy an unusual spot above the round headlights. None of it is showy, but nor does it lack neatness.

AutoVaz did have some design constraints in the Niva's development. The company made the decision to give the car chassis-less, monocoque construction for less workmanlike driving characteristics than previous Russian off-roaders like the Uaz, but to give it adequate innate strength it used plenty of steel, the hefty perimeter structure necessitating a tailgate with a ridiculously high sill; heavy luggage almost had to be craned in. The interior, too,

A right-hand-drive Niva for the British market, opposite, provides proof of the car's international appeal. The car's lines, left, are plain but neatly executed. Capabilities like this, above, have meant the basic Niva is still a strong seller in rural Russia even after twenty-eight years.

was pretty basic on the original model, and mostly adapted from the standard Lada sedan, itself based on the elderly Fiat 124.

An all-new Niva, sometimes sold as a Chevrolet, was shown as a prototype in 1996, finally going into production in 2002. In styling, it is a second-rate attempt at the sector dominated by the Land Rover Freelander and Suzuki Vitara. It is sold at a premium to the old Niva, which of course has meant the former car remains in strong demand. So much so, indeed, that in 2000 AutoVaz launched the Niva L, a long-wheelbase five-door version that, like all Nivas, now has the "luxury" of a hatchback that opens to floor level. Fortunately, in the creation of this rugged derivative, none of the Niva's age-defying, starchy purposefulness has been lost. The Niva remains a very welcome sight right across the steppes.

This view, opposite top, shows Niva's rather limited hatchback third door. Fancy graphics and accessories were introduced for a British-market limited edition, opposite bottom. This French-market Niva, left, sports redesigned bumpers and side skirts, but it is little improvement on the no-frills design honesty of the unadorned car, as shown below.

Jeep Cherokee/ Grand Cherokee

The Jeep Cherokee was a true turning point in car design and a defining moment in SUV history. It was built from 1984 until 2001, so it's most likely that, after the Willys Jeep-type vehicles, the architecture of which was defined by fighting requirements, it is also the Jeep of worldwide popular imagination.

The Cherokee was the first four-wheel drive vehicle from the USA to abandon the traditional construction method of a strong, ladder-like chassis on to which a separate body structure was bolted. This system, going back to the dawn of automotive time, very much suited the

industry because it was tried and tested and gave excellent economies of scale: several different vehicles could be offered all using an identical frame underneath. The body-on-chassis format was not so good for customers, however. The frame had to be extremely heavy since it was the principal load-bearing item, and SUVs so-built—mostly derived from pickups that would be used for slow-moving commercial duties—sometimes proved to be dangerous in the hands of former car drivers, especially those who felt that the commanding driving position afforded by an SUV somehow offered them protection in accidents. Of course,

it was all down to the driver, but truck-based SUVs usually had a high center of gravity and a lot of weight to bring to a halt in an emergency. On top of all this, the heavy chassis construction meant old-style SUVs from Ford and General Motors (as well as Jeep's own aging Wagoneer) had a monstrous thirst for fuel.

Indeed, in a quest to devise an SUV that would offer decent economy, Jeep assigned to two of the world's finest automotive engineers the task of creating the Cherokee. They were Roy Lunn, who had spearheaded Ford's GT40 Le Mans racing program in the 1960s, and François Castaing, a French former Renault engineer

who had worked on many European best-sellers. Neither man wanted to produce a crude gas-guzzler in the Ford Bronco or Chevy Blazer mold.

The breakthrough came with Lunn and Castaing's "Uniframe" integral construction of body and chassis, which made the entire welded structure of the shell bear the weight of the car. Freeing it of the steel girder millstone frame of, say, a Jeep Wagoneer, the designers were able to give the Cherokee four doors in a compact and boxy shape while also giving plenty of curvature to the bodysides, leading to a square-cut, low-roofed glasshouse. A wide track means protruding, square-rigged wheel-arches, the established edged line of which continues beneath the front bumper to form an

Jeep's Cherokee, opposite, unveiled in 1984, established the "boxy" profile that has since been widely copied. The Liberty replacement, right and below, is a less strident statement of modern "Jeepness."

airdam. A bluff front end with a wide grille sports seven wide slats and the rectangular headlights that were ubiquitous in the USA at the time. The entire rear facet of the car is a lightweight tailgate, an almost vertical panel extending right down to floor level.

Aside from its neat packaging (and despite the rather tight interior space), the Cherokee saw massive success thanks to two more features. The base engine initially offered was a thrifty 2.5-liter four-cylinder that, nonetheless, gave a good performance because of the then-exotic fitment of power-boosting fuel injection. And the car's roadholding, due to the years of pooled experience in Lunn and Castaing, was excellent. Accident rates proved the Jeep was just about as safe and as unlikely to roll over as any standard US sedan.

Its appealing compact size put the Cherokee on suburban American drives like no SUV before it. In 1984 Jeep sold 154,801 vehicles; by 1989 that total was up to 249,870—the increase accounted for entirely by surging demand for

the snappily designed, easy-to-drive, compact four-door Cherokee. Further proof of the shifting demographic of SUV buyers was provided by the color palette choice of customers. Jeep had anticipated painting most of the cars in the light, metallic shades preferred in the southern states; in the end, it was inundated with requests for chic darker colors as orders flooded in from coastal areas and, especially, New York. It seemed the Cherokee had singlehandedly taken Jeep from a depressingly low-tech backwater right on to Fifth Avenue.

The new Jeep parent company, Chrysler, did not have it all its own way for long. In 1990, Ford finally retorted with its one-size-larger Explorer. The Explorer, however, didn't bother with the Cherokee's advanced integral build but stuck to a traditional pickup-derived chassis. Happily for Jeep, Castaing responded with the 1993 Grand Cherokee, previewed as the Concept 1 at the 1989 Detroit Auto Show. This larger Cherokee model used the same Uniframe concept, and skid pan tests put it into BMW and Mercedes-Benz sedan territory for controllable road manners.

Importantly, though, the Grand Cherokee offered a bigger, more luxurious cabin within a broader, longer, but still recognizably Jeep (principally from its seven-slat grille Cherokee) overall package. However, the vehicle presents a more dartlike stance, its glasshouse pulled back for a rear bias and its roofline rising to a high point above the C-pillar. A prominent crease in the bodywork, something like the fenderline of a 1960s beach buggy, produces the visual effect of a thick sill/wheelarch structure on which the upper section of an aerodynamic station wagon enjoys a cushioned ride.

The Grand Cherokee proved an even bigger influence on competitors' thinking than the Cherokee and, with the option of V8 engines in upscale models for the first time, Jeep had another hugely successful product on its hands.

The Jeep Grand Cherokee shown on these pages was introduced in 1993 and became an instant hit. Its carlike road manners made it easy for drivers to make the switch from conventional premium sedans.

Rayton Fissore Magnum

The Magnum burst onto the scene with more of a patrician design heritage than any SUV seen up to that point—and probably since. It was the work of Tom Tjaarda, an American-Italian legend in car design. His own father, John Tjaarda, was an acclaimed car stylist from the profession's earliest years in the 1920s, a visionary talent whose experimental, wind-cheating designs led to the Lincoln Zephyr of 1937—the first car in America to make a decent commercial fist of aerodynamic styling. In the 1940s, John Tjaarda was also closely involved in the creation of the handsome, influential lines of the Packard Clipper.

Tom Tjaarda followed in his father's footsteps. After graduating in industrial design, he moved in 1959 to Italy, then the worldwide Mecca of automotive design. Through stints with design houses such as Ghia and Pininfarina, Tjaarda was the designer of such classic sports cars as the Fiat 124 Spider, the Ferrari 330 GT 2+2 and 365 California, and the DeTomaso Pantera. His 1972 Ghia "Project Wolf" economy car went on to global stardom as the first Ford Fiesta in 1976. In 1980, he ended a spell with Fiat by moving to a small coachbuilder outside Turin called Rayton Fissore, and it was here that the man who had created some of the finest Ferraris set to work on his first SUV.

For its new vehicle Rayton Fissore had secured a supply of chassis from Iveco, which used them to make an extremely tough four-wheel drive military vehicle. Compared with the Jeep Cherokee, then, it was a technologically retrograde step, but Tjaarda more than compensated for that in style terms, endowing the Magnum with the sort of spare, tall looks that had recently won the Fiat Uno the European Car of the Year award. Tjaarda had a completely blank sheet of paper on which to work. "I wanted to break away from the typical truck-like appearance," he recalled in *Automobile Quarterly*. "Back then everything was very square, with a ponderous feel. I wanted the Magnum to have a chic and elegant appearance, something with soft curves."

Tjaarda's initial concept sketches won approval from Rayton Fissore owner Giuliano Malvino, and Tjaarda then turned them into detailed renderings and a full-size clay model, working almost single-handedly in a tiny studio. The end result was extraordinarily accomplished and hid the car's inevitable bulk admirably, but during the design process Tjaarda wasn't always confident: "It was a slow process because the radii of a truck are so much bigger than a car—particularly the width. It was critical to get the dimensions right to ensure the proportions would be right."

Although a small enterprise, the Magnum was an instant hit and sold well in the late

Sharp, elegant styling both inside and out was Tom Tjaarda's objective for the Magnum: any trucklike traits were abolished. The car shown here is one of the first Magnums, dating from 1985.

The Magnum was sold in the USA under the LaForza brand, with an interior, right, that was even more luxurious than usual. From this view, below, the Magnum looks merely like a large family wagon with Fiat Uno overtones. An Iveco military-derived chassis gave the Magnum rough terrain guts, opposite top. Rayton Fissore pitched the car at the high-flying lifestyle of the Range Rover owner, opposite bottom.

1980s, eventually coming to the United States rechristened the LaForza and given a typically American power boost with the fitment of a 5-liter Ford Mustang V8 engine (European editions had 2.5-liter Iveco turbodiesel or 2-liter Alfa Romeo gas engines). Sadly, after a few years, sales waned and the capital needed for development dwindled. The Magnum is still made but only in tiny numbers and as a highly specialized vehicle that comes with armor plating as standard. It has dated in one major way: today's SUVs wear their off-road abilities on the outside in the form of manly, muscular-looking surface forms. In this company, the Magnum is unfashionably delicate and, as intended, blandly elegant. But happily, Tjaarda is still hard at work as one of Turin's most in-demand freelance car designers.

Jeep Wrangler

The Jeep is dead—long live the Jeep. The venerable CJ got the ax in 1987 amid much end-of-an-era wailing, only to be replaced by something that, to most people, looked exactly the same. What was going on here?

It was very unusual for a manufacturer actually to announce the death of a legend. When models are dropped, car manufacturers are normally highly discreet, but on November 27, 1985, Jeep executive vice president Joseph Cappy said that what was now known as the Jeep CJ7—essentially, the direct descendant of the wartime Willys Jeep CJ that had been on sale to the public in an unbroken line since 1945—would be no more. Sure enough, in January 1986, the last one was built.

However, concurrent with that announcement, the Wrangler was unveiled as a 1987 model. Through all his "crocodile tears" tributes to the CJ, Cappy had failed to mention one important issue: the huge growth of SUV ownership in the 1970s and 80s had brought an increasing accident rate, especially among young drivers of secondhand vehicles, and the CJ's tall, narrow stance and bouncy leaf-spring suspension had tended to make it more susceptible to toppling over than some other vehicles. The Wrangler represented a chance to begin a new chapter in the Jeep story.

As a consequence, the Wrangler retained the basic passenger "tub" of the CJ—the main metal structure from the windshield back—but sat it on a new chassis that was longer and wider and that positioned the body a little closer to the ground. These dimensions were all a matter of a few inches' difference (although the wheelbase remained the same), but they vastly improved roadholding, as did a coil-

Despite the various states of trim and accessories adorning the Wranglers shown on these pages, the historical Jeep shape and details remain remarkably close to the Second World War original.

sprung chassis frame. A 250-lb. (113-kg) weight increase also helped keep the car anchored to the ground.

The design changes were comprehensive and sometimes puzzling. Rear wheelarches now had a squared-off aperture shape for the first time, to match the Cherokee, while the broader, flatter front mudguards now extended forward to narrow the traditional gap between them and the substantial, girder-like front bumper. The strange part was the trademark grille. In place of the CJ's iconic flat panel with its seven vertical ventilation slats together with a large circular headlight on either side (and a smaller circular direction indicator light set below each), the Wrangler had a "waterfall"-style grille with a kink across the center, flanked by rectangular headlights.

The Wrangler altered the face of the recognizably "Jeep"-shaped vehicle in what was clearly a defiant corporate statement about a new era, although it was also a pointlessly alienating move for Jeep's loyal customers, who generally didn't like it. The proof came in 1997, when Jeep parent Chrysler instigated a meek return to the original style frontage.

As the Wrangler can now trade convincingly on its heritage by being a dead ringer for the revered original, it continues year after year largely unchanged. This is one car that would never benefit from the seasonal facelift imposed on less august motoring fare. However, recent Jeep concept cars have explored the idea of using the Wrangler as a return to more utilitarian models such as a four-door hardtop aimed at the emergency services and a long-wheelbase pickup with a side-mounted spare wheel. Either of these would return Jeep to the four-wheel drive truck market it vacated in 1992 when the Cherokee-based Comanche was deleted.

The 1987 Wrangler, top, did away with the typically Jeep circular headlights, but ten years later the trademark lights returned, right, along with a simpler grille shape and repositioned indicator lights.

The "antidesign" aspect of the Jeep Wrangler is best shown at the rear, above, where the spare wheel, door hinges, and simple taillight clusters hint strongly at a vehicle built to work. Wranglers are ideal for tough terrain, left, but in reality, how many get the chance?

Fiat Panda 4x4 · Volkswagen Golf Country · Peugeot 505 Dangel

Here we look at the curious case of the European family cars that were elevated to meet the rising SUV challenge and to satisfy an important mid-European market where road driving ability in bad weather is a key issue. This, of course, is the mountainous Alpine region that straddles Austria, Switzerland, France, and Italy, a part of the world where an everyday car must be capable of dealing with snow and ice, and where not everyone can afford a Range Rover.

The local need for a cheap and nimble four-wheel drive vehicle had been recognized by Austria's Steyr-Daimler-Puch in 1958 when it launched its Haflinger, an extraordinary, pure utility vehicle aimed at hill farmers. However, it wasn't really a car as such—most came as open buggies—and was too noisy and unrefined, with a 700 cc air-cooled engine in the back, to double up as regular passenger road transport.

It took the launch of Fiat's brilliant, Giorgetto Giugiaro-styled Panda economy car in 1980 to spur SDP into action to produce a small hatchback with all-wheel drive for the tens of thousands of potential customers eager for such a model.

There was plenty of space inside the Panda's cubic, flat-surfaced shape to install the four-wheel drive hardware. External identity is provided by an increased ride height for better ground clearance, the fitment of knobbly tires, and the treatment of the lower panels of the car, which from the wheelarch-top level downward

Already a Giorgetto Giugiaro design classic, the Panda gained its four-wheel drive system thanks to Austria's Steyr-Daimler-Puch, after Fiat deftly grasped the potential for such a car with Alpine-dwelling buyers.

are sheathed in tough, scratch-resistant plastic, making them easy to clean and more rust-resistant. The Panda 4x4 went on sale in 1984 and was an immediate sales star, although with the arrival of a similarly conceived rival from Japan, the Subaru Justy, many Swiss buyers migrated to the Justy for its superior build quality.

Nonetheless, anyone who owned a Panda was stuck with a cramped and slow economy car, so SDP next turned its attention to something a size up, and a paragon of midsize family car style: the Volkswagen Golf. Or, rather, it developed the Syncro four-wheel drive system, with a viscous coupling to engage automatically the rear wheels when they detected that extra traction would be a good idea. This technology was then traded with Volkswagen in exchange for engines and components for other SDP projects; the four-wheel drive Golf Syncro was manufactured in Germany. However, this was merely an all-wheel drive sedan, and so SDP devised something rather more serious: the Golf Country.

SPD built eight thousand Golf Countries, and if you see one you will be immediately struck by the bizarre figure this Golf strikes with its lofty stance. This is thanks to an additional subframe attached underneath the car, which lifts the bodywork some 7 in. (18 cm) above ground level and so boosts the ground clearance over a normal Golf by 2.38 in. (6 cm). An industrial-looking bullbar and a sump guard protect the spotlamp-adorned nose, there are running boards under the doors, and on the back the spare wheel sits in a sling mounted on the hatchback.

Despite its odd appearance, the Country was a sellout in 1990/91 around the Alps. In its official corporate history, Volkswagen comes straight to the point: "Naturally it could not be regarded as an out-and-out all-terrain vehicle but it's often meant all the difference in terms of mobility to its owner when negotiating poor roads or mild off-road sections. Women tended to like it too, because of its commandingly high driving position and the convenience of its four doors." The company is probably right, but the Country was never replaced.

In France, meanwhile, Automobiles Dangel had already been engaged in a similar enterprise for ten years, serving a predominantly French and North African clientele. Its attentions were focused on Peugeot products, with its main output consisting of high-riding, four-wheel drive conversions of the Peugeot 504 pickup and J5 van. In 1986 it added a thoroughly engineered 4x4 conversion of the cavernous Peugeot 505 wagon. As well as its jacked-up ride height—thanks to a substantially modified underframe, which gave tremendous approach and departure angles for traversing, say, a boulder-strewn riverbed—Dangel pumped up the normally elegant Pininfarina-penned 505 lines with bulging black plastic wheelarch extensions to cover the thick, knobbly tires the car wore. Twelve hundred Dangel 505s were made, although by the time of the 505's demise in 1992, French buyers could choose from a variety of purpose-built SUVs that had simply not existed in 1981. Plus, of course, Peugeot now offered its own, rather tamer-looking 405 four-wheel drive wagon. Today, Dangel (still based in the Alsace region of eastern France near the Swiss border) converts Peugeot Partner and Citroën Berlingo vans and wagons to four-wheel drive.

Familiar as these three cars already looked when they were announced, they had an undeniable appeal with their raised ride height and lifestyle-enhancing styling changes. For the child in all of us, they bestow an aura of toys-made-real, but in design terms they are very much yesterday's news.

The Volkswagen Golf Country, below, cut a bizarre motoring figure with its raised platform chassis. Automobiles Dangel transformed the Peugeot 505 estate, opposite, into an elevated cross-country holdall.

Ford Explorer

Unfortunately, the Ford Explorer still has a whiff of notoriety to it, thanks to the involvement of the vehicle in a late 1990s scandal over accidents partly caused by its Firestone tires, and the blizzard of lawsuits that followed the deaths allegedly caused by them. There is no point in trying to avoid mentioning it.

Yet the matter overshadowed one of the most successful product launches in motoring history. The Explorer, when it was first launched in 1990 as a 1991 model, was a smash hit. Just a month after the July launch, Ford SUV sales were up 84%, and by March the following year the

Explorer had grabbed the number seven total sales slot in the USA, and been crowned the country's top-selling "compact" SUV. Its total sales for 1991 were 282,837—an amazing feat considering that its predecessor, the Bronco II, had managed only 122,086 in its best year, 1988.

One key reason was the Explorer's price: $11,000 for a five-door model against $13,500 for the equivalent Jeep Cherokee. But the pluralistic nature of the Ford brand and marketing machine also helped. Suburban American families had an appetite for tough and practical four-wheel drive vehicles that had been whetted by the Cherokee; now here was

an offering from good old Ford that they could actually attain.

"Chunky" is the epithet that best describes the Explorer. A simple, smooth-cornered, two-box outline, with a short front and a long rear overhang, is set off by plastic lower panels all round. A cross-hatched chrome grille with stacked light clusters on either side presents a

The Explorer, shown here in its 1996/97 guise for the British market, was a wildly successful product for Ford. Its lack of progressive engineering was more than made up for by its great-value package.

The excellent occupant visibility, above, and commanding driving position, right, of the Explorer helped it, in Ford's words, "blur the traditional distinctions between cars and trucks."

bluff, oblong face to the world, while a generous glasshouse gives deep windows all round and a high seating position. There is little of the chiseled look of the Cherokee. Nor was there the technical innovation. Unlike the "Uniframe" Cherokee, the Explorer rode on the separate chassis of the Ford pickup line as before and, consequently, was an extremely lucrative venture for Ford. When Ford's divisional general manager Thomas Wagner stated in 1991 that "It is blurring the traditional distinctions between cars and trucks," he wasn't quite correct. But another of his statements— "The Explorer is turning heads in the marketplace"—was absolutely on target. The vehicle turned even more heads after 1995, when the Explorer received an all-new front to make it look more aerodynamic; a sloping hood, curved fenders, and a grille with a rounded, gaping mouth did wonders to relieve the Explorer's endemic trucklike bulk.

The Explorer, which is still an important element of the Ford lineup albeit in a more svelte-looking form, will be remembered for the way it helped the SUV market grow exponentially. It broke little new ground but, in the tradition established by the Model T, was in the vanguard of a new kind of automotive egalitarianism. Still, it's a shame about those tires.

The Explorer, right, is a large passenger vehicle by any standards, but its bulk was disguised with a lowered hood line and gaping "mouth" grille in 1995. Today's version, below, is slightly sleeker still.

Land Rover Discovery

Throughout the frenetic pace of world-wide SUV development during the 1980s, Europe generally maintained a radio silence as the airwaves were dominated by US and Japanese channels. Even the isolated local "station" of Land Rover, purveyor of indomitable transport to the world's armies and maker of the exclusive Range Rover, failed to make much of a bleep. Until, that is, 1989 and the launch of the Land Rover Discovery.

It's highly likely that if Europe had continued to restrict sales of imported Japanese cars, the Discovery might never have happened. However, with Japanese companies building factories to make cars locally in the UK, there was plenty of "quota space" left in their import

The Discovery, this page and opposite bottom left, was a radical departure for Land Rover in 1989. The all-new Discovery, opposite top and bottom right, blends the freshness of the original with a confident and more geometric image.

allocations for cars like the Toyota Land Cruiser, the Isuzu Trooper, and especially the Mitsubishi Pajero. As they all offered cut-rate, excellent quality Range Rover alternatives, Land Rover was stung out of its slumber.

With the Rover Group being perennially strapped for development funds, its off-road contender wasn't entirely new. It shared the Range Rover's separate chassis and its construction method of using mostly aluminum body panels. But there the similarity ended.

In a world of off-road clones, Land Rover's design studio found an individual direction for its compact SUV. Surprisingly, in view of the wild popularity of the five-door Cherokee and Explorer in the USA, the Discovery was initially offered only as a three-door. It has a rearward bias to its styling created by the heavily stepped roof panel that rises abruptly just above the rear quarter-window before terminating at the upright tail; there is a corresponding kink in the bottom line of the rear tailgate window, although it is mostly obscured by the spare wheel and its mounting bracket. Unlike the Range Rover, the Discovery has a side-opening door at the back rather than a horizontally split tailgate.

The raised rear roof section allows a curved glass pane to be installed in its top edge on either side, the line of which, interrupted by the cant rail, is carried down the bodyside to create a deep side window for the luggage area. The other windows, from the windshield round to the rear quarter-window, are united as a visual unit by matt black paint on the A- and B-pillars.

The overall impression is of a tall and narrow car, with a somewhat characterless appearance due to the rather undecided approach to the frontal treatment combined with a black grille and bumper that merge into one. The interior, however, benefited from some lateral thinking thanks to the involvement of the Conran Design consultancy, hence the neat touches of a portable shoulder bag between the two front seats and a pouch behind the driver's seat to hold the removable glass panels over the driver's and front passenger's heads. The use of light blue and green colors in the cabin, in place of the usual gray, also gave it a lift, and made the Range Rover's driver interface seem positively antiquated by comparison.

A five-door model and a belated sales push in the USA followed, and the car was given a comprehensive styling overhaul in 1998. It amounted to a near-total re-skin of the exterior. All of the original Discovery's proportions and cues were retained, however, except for a longer rear overhang so that two extra front-facing seats could be fitted,

The rear quarter-window rising into the roof panel, top, is a Discovery trademark. The central "stack" on the fascia of the latest car, left, makes for a clean-lined interior.

and the Discovery could catch a toehold in the multipurpose vehicle sector that was then burgeoning.

An all-new Discovery was launched in 2004, a bolder, broader, less hunched-up looking car that nonetheless salutes the first Discovery by adopting its stepped roofline and a rear quarter-window that stretches up and over the roof parapet; this is now a single piece of glass bonded over the top of the cant rail metalwork. Proportionally, the new Discovery is very different: Its prominent, semicircular wheelarches are finished in black to give the vehicle a squat air, and the luggage area has adopted the appearance of the hardtop section of a four-door pickup utility. The new Discovery also has razored edges to the hood, giving a sharpness that the old car never possessed.

It's interesting that Land Rover has stuck with the Discovery name. It was unusual in 1989 to go for such a tongue-twisting title; the usual practice is to choose something inoffensively international, which is why this automotive Esperanto throws up such meaningless words as Nubira, Fiero, and Zafira. Discovery was selected for Rover Group by the Interbrand consultancy as part of a program that saw the original Land Rover vehicle renamed the Defender and the later small Land Rover SUV christened Freelander. "We were looking at a more thematic route," recalled Interbrand deputy chairman Tom Blackett. "We wanted to find something that looked rugged both on the page and as you said it. The results were Discovery, Defender, and Freelander ... and several others that have been put aside for possible future use."

The 2004 Discovery, top, builds on the solid fan base of the original car, the black wheelarches giving a more terrain-hugging appearance. Early design sketches, above, suggested a three-door car, but this has not been launched to the public so far.

Daihatsu Feroza

What a wholly unlikely innovator the Feroza is—the long-forgotten pioneer of the small SUV world, which brought recognizably carlike driving characteristics and sparkling performance to the important sector it created. In those early days (1988), it was perhaps unfortunate that Daihatsu opted to shrink the styling of its existing off-road vehicle, the Rocky, around this innovative new package. Most consumers barely recognized it as a separate and very different model. Calling the vehicle the Feroza in Japan and some other markets helped differentiate it, but the Fourtrak and Sportrak titles adopted elsewhere were confusing. Daihatsu might have done better by sticking to the car's codename: "X190 4x4 Leisure Vehicle."

The box-section separate chassis of the Feroza was derived from that of the Rocky,

although it was much shorter in wheelbase and given independent front suspension by torsion bars rather than the cart springs employed by the Rocky for its rural, stump-pulling activities.

A tapering hood, more tumblehome to the bodyside profile, and a basic configuration as a "Targa" style convertible with a substantial fixed rollover hoop, removable roof panel, and drop-down rear soft-top set the Feroza apart from the burly, angular Rocky. The hardtop version was created by substituting a fixed roof section for the canvas hood. Still, to the casual

The 1987 "X190 4x4 Leisure Vehicle," opposite top, is emblazoned with its novel engine message. Bertone's Freeclimber version is pictured opposite bottom. The two vehicles on this page bear the English-market Sportrak branding.

observer, the two cars still looked all but identical, although the Feroza was always far more compact than its bigger forebear. It is also a more eager-looking vehicle, seemingly leaning forward to lap up the terrain ahead, an appearance that is assisted by a sloping swage line that rises gently as it runs back toward its termination spot at a midpoint of the tall, narrow rear light clusters. This feature also acted as the dividing line between the darker upper color and the lighter lower one on some of the two-tone paint schemes offered as an option.

A peppy performance came from the Feroza's sixteen-valve engine; it was the first off-roader ever to offer this multivalve engine

Despite Daihatsu's intentions, the Feroza was always more accomplished off the road than on it, right. It is pictured below in convertible guise. The Feroza/Sportrak in open and closed forms, opposite, tapped into the lifestyle and leisure time made possible by 1980s affluence.

technology, which had enlivened the "hot hatchback" genre. Unlike with the Rocky, there was no diesel.

The Feroza/Sportrak was always intended as something of a self-consciously chic urban runabout. Most contemporary pundits, paradoxically, found it quite capable off-road but mediocre on, thanks to a noisy engine that delivered its power unevenly, and seats that were uncomfortable on long journeys. But the geometric, blocky look quickly proved a turn-off to buyers when the more accessible Suzuki Vitara came along, and sales dwindled. Even a tie-up with venerable Italian design house Bertone, which built the Feroza in Italy and offered it as the Bertone Freeclimber with some interestingly different two-tone paint jobs, could not help. The Feroza/Sportrak was ultimately a correct prediction of where the market was heading, but executed in the wrong way. In trying to miniaturize the look of the agricultural 4x4 establishment, Daihatsu narrowly misjudged the consumer mindset. That, once again, is maybe why Daihatsu is rarely credited for kick-starting the small SUV revolution.

Suzuki Vitara/X-90

With the 1989 Vitara, Suzuki proved it had come an enormously long way since establishing itself as a maker of tiny four-wheel drive vehicles in 1970 with the Jimny. By the late 1980s, the limitations of that car in terms of performance, comfort, and styling had truly been reached, although there was still a ready market for it for both agricultural/industrial and leisure applications. A few people were even willing to endure the Jimny every day for commuting, but they tended to be hardy individualists.

So the Vitara was brilliantly conceived as a 4x4 with priority given to on-road user-friendliness. Its design was visual accessibility itself. Suzuki took the proportions of a super-mini and pumped them up so that the Vitara has a tall glasshouse. The frontal area, however, is kept small, tapered, and drawn around the components within, while blistered wheel-arches give the requisite solidly planted track without the slab-sided bulk of, say, a Ford Bronco II.

Once inside, it's hard to imagine the Vitara is a mud-plugger, with its sports car-like, body-hugging seats, a dashboard that curves away from the driver, and an interesting contrast between light seat upholstery and door panels and dark plastic trim. One novel touch is a dip in the window line just in front of the rearview mirror, adding interest to the side profile and letting more light into what is already an airy interior. The side-opening rear door with exterior-mounted spare wheel is practical, while for those people wanting open-air fun, Suzuki also produced a separate convertible model.

The fact that the Vitara was best suited to light off-road duties, with front-wheel drive most of the time, didn't matter. It was good to drive on the road and, because its design was among the first to make a fundamental attempt to cross over into the car sector—blurring the traditional divides of the rigidly segmented

automotive market—it was a favorite with consumers. Its success was underscored after General Motors got wind of the project and marketed it through US Chevrolet dealers as the Geo Tracker.

The Vitara has matured and evolved since then, although no subsequent versions have

made so much impact on the market or on the car design fraternity. One Suzuki that did cause a stir, however, was the X-90. It was one of the most daring launches in recent times. The X-90 resulted from a recognition that there was a large number of single drivers and couples with disposable incomes who would naturally

Unlike the Daihatsu Feroza, which just predated it as the world's first small SUV, the Suzuki Vitara, right, was offered in completely separate wagon and convertible versions from the outset.

The five-door Vitara, left, proved a great way to enjoy a family-sized SUV with low running costs. Suzuki cultivated a self-consciously "cool" image for the Vitara, below.

plump for a pure sports car but who felt the gravitational pull of the new SUV movement. The rationale was to offer a two-seater "sporty" car with four-wheel drive but with SUV proportions.

This sort of "fun car" had been widely proposed before as motor show concepts by many companies and, true to form, Suzuki first revealed the Vitara-based X-90 at the Tokyo Motor Show in 1991 as merely a design exercise. However, unlike its rivals, the company had real faith in this novel motoring format, and the car went on sale five years later.

The X-90's lines are softer than the Vitara's, with more rounded bulges to its fenders, while the turret-like two-seater glasshouse comes with twin removable glass panels to open up the vehicle on those endless, hot Californian days. Elliptic headlights set up its smooth contours at the front, with the waistline pulling back to a rounded little rump featuring a conventional opening trunk lid topped by a rear spoiler—a rather unnecessary aerodynamic device bearing in mind that the X-90 struggled to its 93 mph (150 kph) top speed. It was more of a car for posing than performance, and if that was pretentious then this was as pretentious as it got.

If that was the sort of car you'd always yearned for, then here, at last, was the real thing ready to be driven. In fact, the market proved elusive, with just 7246 vehicles sold in the X-90's primary market, the USA, in two years, another 1500 going to the UK, some sold in Japan, and a few more elsewhere. Total sales can have been no more than twenty thousand—a drop in the SUV ocean even by the standards of the relatively small Suzuki.

Slightly dispiriting, too, was the critical reaction to the X-90. Journalists had spent years berating manufacturers for exhibiting interesting show cars while offering cautious, predictable fare to the public. Now Suzuki did something tangentially different, and it was derided for the end result in a way that would never greet the unveiling of a 200-mph supercar. The X-90 has been remorselessly criticized for what it was not—a fully functioning and practical SUV; perhaps now we should recognize its status as the much-maligned pioneer of sport utility vehicle hybrids in which the sporty element comes to the fore in recognition of our changing demographics.

A very early photograph of the first Vitara, opposite top, shows the clever detailing. The radical X-90, opposite bottom, was the world's first SUV/two-seater sports car hybrid. The latest Vitara five-door, below, with its bulging, organic lines, lacks the crispness of the original.

SsangYong Musso · Kia Sportage · Kia Sorento · SsangYong Rexton

Perhaps bracketing these four designs together is a little unfair, since the main theme that defines them as a group is that they all hail from South Korea. But in any book of this type, editorial judgment has to be exercised. Most readers would probably agree that none of these vehicles represents a profound shift in SUV design thinking. Collectively, however, they prove that a previously nonexistent national motor industry can have a sudden impact on a marketplace. In the same way that the Ford Explorer brought plurality to the US SUV market in 1991, the Koreans represented a cost-effective entry for drivers who, perhaps, had been harboring a desire for one of the smaller Japanese models but were deterred by premium prices.

Before it schemed the Musso, SsangYong had built what were, in essence, naked copies of Jeeps and Mitsubishis. A deal with Mercedes-Benz provided the 2.9-liter diesel engine, while a tie-up with Professor Ken Greenley of London's Royal College of Art meant it could call on some genuine design talent. As one half of the partnership (with John Heffernan) that had created the looks of the Aston Martin Virage, Bentley Continental R, and Panther Solo, Greenley knew how to make an impact, but the challenge with the Musso was in stark contrast.

Greenley discovered that there was a hunger for large SUVs in South Korea in the early 1990s, but that the main emphasis was always on the rear compartment because owners who could afford such a prestigious vehicle were generally chauffeured. He recalled: "I'd put a lot of effort into making the driving position of my first design proposal attractive and BMW-like but the [SsangYong] chairman got into the back of it, turned to me, and said: 'Where are my controls?' It's something I hadn't realized: in the upper echelons of Korean society there's not much interest in what the driver does. The guy who signed the cheque for the car is bothered about where he'll be sitting—in the back. And the car had to tempt the Korean upper bourgeoisie out of their luxury cars."

Greenley also pointed out that it is more important for people to like what they see than understand what it all means: "So this car has two 'halves': the top is vital, it's the bit you see, the bit that's in the presence of other car users—particularly when they're sitting in

The Kia Sorento, below and opposite bottom, is traditional in concept and honors the Mercedes-Benz M-Class for stylistic influence. The SsangYong Musso, opposite top, established (with British help) South Korea's SUV scene; note its station wagon-like topside.

traffic. It is, to all intents and purposes, a passenger car. It's low and turretlike. The bottom half, though, below the waist, is a 4x4, honest to goodness."

The final design, with its modern, station wagon-like topside, turned out to be pretty slippery when Greenley tested models of it in the March racing car team wind tunnel: "I wasn't aiming for a low Cd [coefficient of drag] figure but really for less wind noise. I'd learned working on Bedford trucks that if you get that on a big, boxy shape, you also tend to get a lot of dirt deposition. You've got to keep a truck clean for safety reasons and, with an off-roader, the principle is the same if it's going to be splashing through mud. By tapering the body as you would a normal [sedan] car, we got rid of a lot of wind noise."

Second-string Korean newcomer Kia joined the SUV fray in 1994 with its Sportage, a rather less accomplished mélange of ideas. Kia's lack of brand identity was not helped by the anonymously rounded form of the

Sportage, with its uncomfortable ratio of frontal area—a hood line dropping away from the driver as in a city car—to the lump of a passenger compartment looking like a giant loaf of bread. It was a "soft-roader" in the manner of the five-door Suzuki Vitara, but one executed in an unconvincing manner.

The Sportage was joined in February 2002 by a larger, full-size (by European/Japanese standards, "compact" as the USA would have it) stablemate, the Kia Sorento. A rugged, authentic SUV, the Sorento features straightforward ladder-frame chassis construction with double-wishbone front suspension and multilink rear suspension, a long wheelbase, and a wide track. At the back is a split-opening tailgate. It's a great-value package, but the styling, in proportion, forms, and even some details, is so similar to the top-selling Mercedes-Benz M-Class—surely no coincidence—that the Sorento barely makes an impression on the SUV design envelope, much less pushes it.

The first Kia Sportage, above, was a rather insipid small SUV in the Toyota RAV4 idiom. SsangYong's Rexton, right and opposite, is a mishmash of themes taken from existing passenger cars, but its destiny is now in Chinese hands.

A final offering is the Rexton, designed by Italdesign. It may be a feast for the eyes, but it can lead to a bout of visual indigestion. At the front, Ford's "Edge Design" principle of bisecting styling curves defines the grille and slanted headlights, while the rear three-quarter aspect, with its diagonally upswept D-pillar and wrap-around, triangular rear corner windows, is pirated from the Mercedes-Benz A Class. Enormously bulging wheelarches draw the eye to the car's huge, toylike spoked alloy wheels. To dismiss the Rexton would be foolhardy, however. Control of SsangYong has recently passed to Shanghai Automotive Industry Corporation and, thus, it has become the first global car brand under Chinese direction. The future design developments of a newly empowered SsangYong will be fascinating to watch.

Isuzu VehiCROSS

The discussion earlier in this book of the Suzuki X-90 and its remarkable transition from show car to showroom might give the impression that such a genesis is bound to end in critical failure. Not at all; in the early 1990s, the process was unheard of but, by the decade's end, it had become the industry norm for a manufacturer first to reveal a concept model and then, lo and behold, to confirm it for production shortly afterward as an outward sign of what a progressive organization it was. The Mercedes-Benz SLK and Ford Ka are good examples. This practice could easily be

dismissed as a cynical strategy, an entirely pre-planned "surprise." The more radical designs, after all, rarely make it to wheel-turning reality without undergoing a thorough watering down.

The Isuzu VehiCROSS is an admirable exception. It caused quite a stir at its 1993 Tokyo Motor Show debut, where it was said to be constructed from carbon fiber and aluminum, provided with four passenger doors, and powered by a 1.6-liter four-cylinder engine. But it caused a storm in 1997 when it went on sale looking, if anything, even more radical.

The impression is of some sort of futuristic amphibious vehicle, or a dune buggy at the very least, the car's painted metalwork (now made of steel) riding on a fluid-looking cushion of black polyurethane. Of course, it's just cladding, but it gives the impression that,

The Isuzu VehiCROSS was the design work of Simon Cox, a graduate of the Royal College of Art in London, who said that he wanted to do something "exciting and seductive" with the SUV, rather than just create a show car.

157

hovercraft-like, it supports the whole car. The main panels suggest a very loose "melted" interpretation of the three-door Isuzu Amigo, with an ultrawide B-pillar. A matt black panel on the hood hints at the nonreflective hoods fitted to rally cars destined for sub-Saharan events, while the side-opening rear door has the outline of the concealed spare wheel molded into it. Particularly stylish are the headlamps, nestling in nacelles embedded midway between the black lower section and the metal hood area, bleeding back to a pointed tip on the hood surface. Inside, German Recaro seats and a small Italian Momo steering wheel

A special edition of the VehiCROSS, above, sports a unique grille, roof bars, and huge chrome wheels. There is something amphibian about the VehiCROSS styling, right.

give the further lie that this is some sort of Paris–Dakar 4x4 off-road rally special. A true technical innovation was a video camera mounted in the back bumper to aid reversing, while a single fender mirror at the front of the passenger-side fender was a further detail to give the VehiCROSS driver excellent all-round visibility.

It's still a shock to see a VehiCROSS in the flesh eight years since it went on sale—alas, only in Japan and the USA as a high-priced, largely hand-built, limited-production model with the Trooper donating the entire 3.2-liter V6 four-wheel drivetrain. The last one was made in 2001 after only 4300 were sold stateside.

A notably international team created this remarkable-looking car, which was intended to be, in Isuzu's official statement, "an emotional recreational vehicle, one that you will care about." The team was led by Satomi Murayama, chief designer/manager at Isuzu's European office in Brussels, with his assistant chief designer being Simon Cox—a quiet young Briton who had come to industry-wide attention while working for Lotus (he penned the interior of the 1988 Elan).

Sponsored by Ford while studying at London's Royal College of Art (RCA), Cox studied jewelry and silversmithing before his postgraduate vehicle design course. He says that 4x4 design really brings out the product designer in him, feeling that these cars need more functional detailing than other types of vehicle. He used this to advantage on the VehiCROSS, maximizing every detail to give additional or specific appeal. In Cox's words:

When you start a production programme you don't want to be doodling around. When a concept car approaches production stages, the financial stakes are high and a concrete pathway is key. The VehiCROSS was never intended to be a production vehicle. I was asked to do a vehicle for the Tokyo show and it was up to me to decide what vehicle we should aim for. What I tried to do was not to make it an "all-singing, all-dancing" show car that people would just take or leave; I wanted it to have some meaning. I wanted to do something exciting and seductive enough to be at a motor show, and attract people's attention, but which had enough meaning to lead to a production vehicle. And it did in the end. Some concept vehicles are purely show cars for glitz and glamour;

The VehiCROSS appears to be riding on a hovercraft-like air cushion, left, although it's actually black plastic cladding. The embedded headlights and black hood are shown to good effect, below. The 1.6-liter prototype, bottom, was revealed at the 1993 Tokyo Motor Show.

some are more styling-orientated, and some are technology-orientated. My personal aim is to do something meaningful. It's a serious endeavour.

Such was Cox's serious-minded talent that he didn't stay at Isuzu for long, becoming in 1998 director of Concept Vehicle Design for General Motors. He was even able to persuade the American multinational to let him base his studio on the bridgehead between the US and European market—the UK—where it could take advantage of the stream of interesting talent coming out of the RCA.

The VehiCROSS, meanwhile, is certain to be a collector's item. Who knows—perhaps it could become the Jaguar E-type or Chevrolet Corvette of the SUV world.

Mercedes-Benz M-Class

Mercedes-Benz could have chosen just about any type of car as its maiden US-built product in 1997, but it selected an all-new design of SUV as the most appropriate. The reason for building a greenfield factory in Tuscaloosa, Alabama, was to expand vastly its global reach, and all the firm's plants located in its traditional domicile of Germany were full to capacity making sedans, wagons, and sports cars. The US venture would be brand new in every sense of the word.

Mercedes did not wish to use its existing G-Wagen as a basis for its SUV. That was not a sport utility vehicle in the modern idiom, and could never be modified as such. An all-new car was absolutely necessary, and it was previewed in the 1996 All-Activity Vehicle (AAV) concept car.

The resulting design for the M-Class set a new benchmark in crossover styling for such a large car, although luckily it ditched the prominent "suggested" separate fenders and lower panels of the AAV; they would have turned out to be far too close to the later BMW X5's lines for comfort. The styling lines all emanate from the parallelogram Mercedes grille with its prominent three-pointed star motif. The faired-in line of the tapered headlights carries the eye up and back over the front fenders; it then rises sharply again in a steeply raked windshield and A-pillar, up and over the roof to end in a kinked drop-down to bumper level just as in a family hatchback like the Volkswagen Golf. Indeed, with nothing around the M-Class to give it scale when viewed from the middle distance, the effect is extremely Golf-like even down to the slightly flared wheelarches and neat, sedan car-like door apertures.

The chief characteristic of the bodyside is a forward-leaning C-pillar that slices through the glasshouse to split the rear-door glass from the quarter-window pane. Standard roof bars that begin just above the windshield and run to the very end of the roof help add sleekness. Plain without being overtly Germanic, the M-Class is chic and neat and just the job for its aspiring market sector. The smart cabin gives

The 1996 AAV (All-Activity Vehicle) concept, below, was a foretaste of the German company's foray into the modern SUV market. In the event, the 1997 M-Class, opposite, was rather more toned-down and true to the make's usual restrained styling ethos.

little clue that this is a car for making mincemeat of tough terrain.

Customer choice is *de rigueur* for Mercedes, and within two years a powerful ML55 AMG V8 option topped the standard 2.7-liter V6, while an economical five-cylinder CDI diesel tailed it. A V8 4-liter diesel was offered in 2002 at the same time as a mild facelift for exterior trim and bumpers.

The M-Class has been a phenomenally successful car, with 140,000 sold in its first two years—many of these sales snatched from the Detroit establishment. It collected no end of consumer magazine accolades, too, plus an important declaration of being "safest car" from the US Insurance Institute for Highway Safety after a series of crash tests. It is probable that hardly any M-Class purchasers were unhappy with their choice, and the model has aged well. Nonetheless, the design of the M-Class is hard

to get really excited about; it makes its prestigious statement calmly and clearly, but communicates little in the way of design passion. This play-it-safe ethos is what has made General Motors's Saturn brand such a winner and, like those unobtrusively designed vehicles, the M-Class has many female buyers on its side. Quite how it will be replaced remains to be seen, but it will be a formidable design challenge to shout in an SUV market where there is so much more product noise than there was in 1997.

As the images on these two pages demonstrate, with nothing near the M-Class to give it scale, it could easily be a large family hatchback in the Golf idiom. The car was a sales phenomenon, with 140,000 delivered to customers in its first two years.

Honda CR-V/HR-V/Pilot

If one were looking for an SUV to single out for making the urban environment a more dangerous place, then the Honda CR-V would be the wrong choice. Thanks to the company's groundbreaking work in designing pedestrian crash-test dummies, it was able to revise the hood and windshield wipers for the second-generation CR-V. This enabled the car, a small SUV built in the UK and Japan, to score an excellent three stars in the Euro NCAP (New Car Assessment Programme) impact tests; it was an unprecedented score for such a four-wheel drive off-roader.

There is no doubt about it: when Honda puts its mind to vehicle design, it generally comes up with winners. They may not always be the flashiest products in their sectors, but they have a deserved reputation for brilliant fulfillment of their intended rôles. Honda was a latecomer to the SUV gathering; realizing its impending importance, indeed, the company bought time by selling the Isuzu Rodeo and Land Rover Discovery under the Honda brand, but when it did launch its own vehicle, the CR-V in 1997, it was a commendably neat, well-executed five-door, high-waisted but with a strong shoulder running front to back, with the glasshouse slightly inset to reduce the impression of bulk. At the front, there was a strong resemblance to other Hondas with a narrow grille and thin headlights, but it was at the back that there was most design interest. A split tailgate featured a lift-up glass upper section but a swing-out lower door. The tailgate also had the novelty of a built-in water tank and shower attachment for, for example, hosing down muddy boots after a country walk or cleaning children's grubby hands. The rear light clusters formed part of the D-pillars for excellent rearward nighttime visibility.

The CR-V was to have been developed on the same platform as the Land Rover Freelander, since the two companies had a joint-venture agreement, but Honda was eventually forced to do all its own work after the accord was quickly unwound when Rover was acquired by BMW. Those who know both parties dispassionately would probably say that was to Honda's advantage. The Japanese company's independence has long been its one key asset.

The 2002 replacement CR-V may have been more pedestrian-friendly, but it is not as svelte, with thicker pillars and a less pronounced shoulder being part of an altogether bulkier-looking car. By that time, Honda's second-string SUV, the HR-V, had joined it. Based on a 1997 Tokyo Motor Show concept called the JWJ

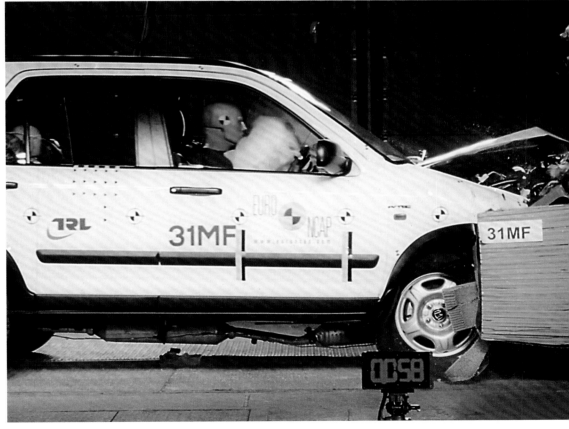

The original CR-V, above, was Honda's first SUV. The 2002 CR-V MkII, opposite, is less harmonious in design but safer on impact. The current CR-V, right, has provided class-leading crash-test results.

(where it was one of a trio exhibited under the banner of "Joy Machines"), the 1999 HR-V is a curious, but not unattractive, amalgam of small, straight-lined wagon and traditional "Jeep Cherokee"-style off-roader, although on a scale even more compact than the CR-V. A pronounced indentation runs around the whole of the car's perimeter at wheelarch-top level, while its wedge-shaped nose exudes Honda's pedestrian-friendliness, with the four headlights concealed behind smoothly contoured plastic covers. The sharply truncated rear end is set off by a hot-roddish roof-mounted spoiler. The HR-V is said to have been a part-time fun project for a team of young Honda designers, and it certainly has a crisply different character; so it must have been dispiriting when it was criticized for not being macho enough, since that was never the intention.

Honda's third off-roader is the Pilot. To tune this larger SUV precisely to US tastes, the car was created at Honda's centers in Ohio and California. Honda engineers went so far as to conduct home visits with potential customers in order to gain a thorough understanding of what they wanted. Said Frank Paluch, Honda R&D chief engineer for the Pilot: "We wanted to improve on those market weak points and also create a smart design that would surpass customer expectations. Altogether, we gave the Honda Pilot the most versatile interior wrapped with traditional SUV rugged toughness and Honda's core values of safety, environmental friendliness, and world-class quality for the ultimate family adventure."

Honda also found that most buyers wanted "medium duty off-road capability"—in other words, the vehicle had to feel good on the road and only get truly bogged down in the worst

kind of quicksand; towing cattle trailers along rutted tracks wasn't really a requirement.

The roomy and versatile "family functional" interior was one thing, but the exterior is redolent of one that has been market-researched to death, which is presumably why there are bits of Lexus RX300, bits of Mercedes M-Class, and bits of the CR-V clearly visible. Honda calls the Pilot the "Ultimate American Family Adventure Vehicle," citing Yosemite National Park and the distinctive Pelican equipment case as disparate sources of inspiration, but it is actually a shrewd cocktail of everything an active middle America wants from its family carryall. There is nothing wrong with that, but it feels as though little of that rare elixir, the car designer's vision, has been deemed useful.

The distinctive HR-V, opposite top and bottom, grew out of a part-time fun project among Honda stylists that created the Joy Machine show car. Unremarkable styling for the Honda Pilot, above and right, was nonetheless just what US customers told researchers they preferred.

Toyota RAV4

The Daihatsu Sportrak and Suzuki Vitara were certainly the mold-breakers in terms of cracking the concept for a mini-SUV in the late 1980s. By comparison with the Toyota RAV4 of 1994, however, even these two accomplished vehicles seem somewhat clumsy in their execution.

It is rare for Japanese manufacturers to allow the name of a designer to be revealed, much less be attached to a particular product. An exception was made for Masakatu Nonaka, the chief engineer and, by the company's own admission, the guiding light behind what became the Recreational Activity Vehicle with four-wheel drive, or RAV4. A figure with a huge standing within Toyota, Nonaka joined the company in 1967 and by 1974 was in charge of product planning for all commercial and recreational vehicles after a spell working on experimental safety systems such as airbags.

In 1986 Toyota established a working group to examine new car products, and by 1988 Nonaka was in charge of the group, guiding the first concept for a compact SUV to its little-noticed unveiling at the 1989 Tokyo Motor Show. He said four-wheel drive vehicles were his passion, along with other outdoor pursuits such as mountain- and trail-biking, but he wasn't convinced that the early concept, with its rigid rear axle and overtly rugged styling, was going to work. So Nonaka set off for a long European fact-finding mission to get a feel for where SUV use was going. Time spent in pavement cafés across Europe, armed only with a cappuccino and a notebook, was not wasted: Nonaka soon realized that younger owners of sport utilities rarely used the "utility" of their cars, and just as rarely indulged in any "sports" with them. Most of the time was spent cruising city boulevards, with a very

occasional trip to the coast as a weekend tonic to the tired urban system.

"This trend wasn't really difficult to pick up," Nonaka said. "In Europe, but also in the US and Japan, it was obvious that young people would want a different type of car in the 1990s. The Toyota RAV4 had to be different from traditional off-roaders and passenger cars. We wanted it to be something completely new and fresh, so a lot of time was spent getting the details right."

Even before the details, however, Nonaka conceived of a construction that was pure, monocoque road car, with high ground clearance, large wheels and tires, and

The Toyota RAV4, below and opposite top, was a watershed in SUV design and engineering. Three- and five-door models of the second-generation RAV4, opposite bottom, were introduced in 2000.

permanent four-wheel drive. A 2-liter, fuel-injected twin-cam engine from the Toyota Camry would give strong performance, while suspension would be tuned for great on-road capability but still robust enough for the odd sojourn off-road—and certainly at ease in slippery conditions or moderately severe terrain. In effect, it would simply be a four-wheel drive road car.

Nonaka's team was then able to massage back in the SUV-style elements that most appealed to customers' imaginations. The high-up driving position was a must, but blocky proportions were junked in favor of an undulating, dune buggy-like fenderline. Lower body panels were toughened with damage-resistant plastic, and the profile was of a low-at-the-front/high-at-the-rear hot rod with a small frontal area, a neat radiator grille as part of the hood, and dynamic sculpted, slanted head-lights. A swing-out rear cargo door has its release handle integrated into the rear lamp cluster, a neat touch, while aluminum roof

panels at the front and rear can be lifted out to create an open car without the need to offer a separate soft-top model.

Once Toyota was satisfied with the unusual design—and it took a lot to persuade the company's conservative management that it would sell—the car went from concept to running prototype in just fifteen months. "Lots of effort went into convincing the right people," Nonaka said.

The RAV4 broke new ground in another way too; revealed in customer-ready form at the 1994 Geneva Motor Show (having been previewed a year earlier at the Brussels event as a near-production concept called the "Fun Cruiser"), it was the first Toyota product ever to have its world premiere in Europe, its key market. It was very definitely touted to the former hatchback driver, after Toyota researchers discovered that 62% of buyers of existing mini-SUVs in Germany were trading in cars like Volkswagen Golfs to get on this trendy new bandwagon.

Indeed, the RAV4 proved an excellent sales performer for Toyota, and the company must have felt quietly smug that it had spent the eight long years between first contemplating the car and finally putting it on sale getting it absolutely on target. The RAV4 was a design landmark that soon spawned a five-door derivative and has been replaced by models that look sharper and more "jagged" yet adhere faithfully to Mr. Nonaka's carefully honed philosophy.

The RAV4 features lift-out aluminum roof panels for open-top driving, opposite top. Graphics and extra spotlights boost the RAV4's jungle-broaching credibility, opposite bottom. The RAV4 MkII, above and right, is certainly a better consumer product, but its styling has become over-elaborate.

Nissan Terrano II · Ford Maverick

Automotive joint ventures have largely vanished since the world motor industry consolidated into just ten major groupings. Furthermore, such ventures are rarely what they seem, since one partner usually holds the whip hand whatever the public pronouncement. So it is likely that Ford would never have planned the Maverick as it turned out but, because the company desperately needed an SUV of its own in 1992 for its European markets—especially because General Motors had already launched its Frontera version of the Isuzu Amigo—it was happy to hook up with Nissan's nearly finished Terrano II enterprise.

Through its acquisition of a Spanish truck plant, Nissan gained an early toehold in the European SUV market by building its Patrol there from the early 1980s. A decade later and it was clearer than ever that the Patrol, robust though it was, was entirely the wrong product in a market where the Suzuki Vitara was being lapped up by buyers.

The Terrano II is a rare shop window for Italian SUV design. Stylists at the IDEA Institute went for a tall, narrow look with an undulating fenderline and a relatively smooth overall impression. Both three- and five-door models are shown here.

Nissan wanted to be absolutely sure it had accurately felt the European pulse of the burgeoning SUV sector, rather than imposing a Japanese or American design on reluctant consumers. This is the reason it called in Italy's IDEA Institute consultancy to handle the styling. IDEA, based in an eighteenth-century villa in the hills outside Turin, had made quite a name for itself. The first project it revealed was the Fiat VSS, a 1980 experimental car to show the feasibility of sharing platforms between different models; it led to the 1989 Fiat Tipo and its seven spin-off sister cars. After a decade of working mostly for Fiat, the Nissan was among the first of IDEA's other design projects.

"We will never build cars," said Franco Mantegazza, who founded IDEA in 1978, "but we do everything from the clean sheet up to the point of manufacture. We call it '360-degree design.'" He added: "Automotive is the key to what we do but we've also designed bicycles, motorcycles, scooters, boats, tractors, buses, lighters, office buildings, and telephones. IDEA stays fresh by doing non-automotive design, which is why the car companies keep coming to us. We are doing 'Bauhaus for automotive.'"

For the Terrano II, IDEA went for the undulating "Coke bottle" fender that was widespread in the late 1960s, to make the basically tall and narrow off-roader shape less offensive. The side profile starts at headlamp level, rising fairly steeply to the windshield base, leveling off and then rising again over the "haunch" of the bulging rear wheelarch. A multifaceted front bumper panel curves around the car's corner to marry up to the thick plastic wheelarch trim, while a squarish hood bulge spreads out just before the windshield base to set up the profile of the A-pillars. It's a smoothly finished overall exercise with none of the usual surface detail of ribs or indentations to communicate built-in strength, although a narrow track imbues it with a slightly top-heavy character.

Twelve years after its launch, the Terrano II is still being made, albeit under the cloak of a frontal facelift. It is capable off-road but not much liked, gaining the dubious accolade of "Britain's worst car" from one respected British motoring magazine. Ford's edition, the Maverick, was launched in 1992 at exactly the same time as the Terrano II (why Nissan selected that name is unclear—the original Terrano, the "I," was not sold in Europe), but it was never marketed with any conviction and was dropped in 2000. So much for joint ventures; the Terrano probably looked its best in drawings in the boardroom of that Torinese villa all those years ago.

Ford Maverick simply means, in a European context, a Nissan Terrano II in "blue oval" livery, and the cars on these pages show both variations. However, the Maverick was discontinued in 2000 when Ford turned instead to Mazda for its re-branded SUV fare.

Subaru Forester

Despite its agricultural title, the Subaru Forester is not a machine for hauling logs. It is a spacious and relatively tall station wagon. For anyone who suffers backache, who has small children, or who's probably just of an age over forty, it must seem a mystery why a station wagon should come in any other size, because the Forester offers masses of head- and leg-room, an adequately authoritative driving position, and a usefully "square" cargo area that can accommodate a large dog in airy comfort or else move the contents of a small apartment in one fell swoop.

For the vast majority of potential buyers, a car with any more ground clearance than the Forester already has—which would manifest itself merely in increased, towering size—would be of no practical use. The Forester is an SUV on a human scale, with only the five seats of a normal station wagon.

The Forester looks most purposeful in its more basic version. Here, the bumpers and lower side panels are in scratch-resistant black plastic, imparting immediately an image of workmanlike grittiness. But the Forester also offers sleek contours, helped especially by a flared rear fender with an extended wheelarch

extension that tapers away toward the car's tail to give the impression it has been blown that way by the wind. An unusual feel to the rear aspect is formed by triangular light clusters, with the tailgate shutline tapering inward between them.

Such is Subaru's take on the SUV genre today. It's maybe surprising that the small

Three views of the current Subaru Forester reveal it as a tall station wagon with excellent ground clearance, the two attributes that make it ideal for the majority of buyers.

Japanese manufacturer makes such a restrained and sensible stab at the car type; after all, since it introduced its first four-wheel drive station wagon in 1973 it stole a march on its rivals that could have easily been exploited with a move up to a more conventional SUV. Instead, Subaru has been a focused proponent of four-wheel drive in conventional road cars. It has an enviable record with these, proven on the World Rally Championship stage. The first WRC event Subaru contested was the 1990 Safari Rally with a four-wheel drive Legacy sedan. It was a good start: the car became the first Group N (that is, very close to production car specification) car ever to complete the Safari. But the more compact Impreza, revealed in November 1992, was the foundation on which the make's rally prowess has been built. In 1995, Subaru achieved overall wins in five of the eight WRC rallies with the Impreza Turbo, making Subaru the WRC Manufacturers' Champion. Subaru then went on to win the title in the following two years, achieving three straight WRC wins from 1995 to 1997—a first for a Japanese carmaker.

Subaru felt that the best way to capitalize on this success was to stick with conventional road cars, such as the first Forester, which entered the market in 1997. The proportions were similar to today's model's, although the rear glasshouse line was more boxy and the side panels were simpler, more planar. Consequently, Subaru has less to shout about in design terms, giving it a much lower SUV profile than, say, Toyota or Suzuki. However, people who know these fantastically well-built cars rather relish their best-kept-secret aura.

SUV-haters would have trouble lambasting the Forester with their "Chelsea tractor" epithet, so carlike are its proportions, left and opposite top. The original 1997 Forester, below and opposite bottom, set the style and basic shape for today's car.

Land Rover Freelander

Every vehicle Land Rover has ever launched seems to be one that carries the entire future of the British four-wheel drive specialist with it. This is manna for headline writers, of course, but a bit tiresome to have to repeat over and over again. Still, we need to do so here because the Freelander, which was introduced at the 1997 Frankfurt Motor Show, was certainly the most radical departure from the Land Rover norm.

At the heart of this was the fact that the Freelander had no separate chassis at all. It was, in effect, a "normal," monocoque-construction road car provided with four-wheel drive and raised ground clearance. As such, it was another "soft-roader" but, unlike the expectations of products from Honda, Kia, et al., this one had the tricky advertising legacy of "The Best 4x4xFar" to take with it. Fortunately, however, critics didn't give it a roasting for its less-than-aggressive appetite for powering its

way through yard-deep swamp, while customers gave it such a positive welcome that the Freelander has been Europe's top-selling SUV since 1999.

This success is in no small part down to the masterful work of Gerry McGovern, the British designer who oversaw the Freelander's winning looks and a graduate from London's Royal College of Art in 1976. McGovern started work on the car—which was codenamed CB40 while under development—shortly after completing the MGF sports car, and his versatility subsequently propelled him to the top design job at Lincoln in the USA.

Instead of slavishly attempting to mimic the bigger, separate chassis Land Rovers, McGovern went for a buggy-ish, high-waisted look that seemed to suggest that the Freelander was nimble enough to bounce across just about anything. Its smoothly contoured lower panels make it look as though it would slither its way

over anything it could not leapfrog. "With most road cars, they're styled," McGovern said at the time. "But working at Land-Rover allows us to be, almost, industrial designers. Vehicles like these have to be usable. Every feature should do a job while conveying what the vehicle can do. Land Rovers have to be robust, solid, go-anywhere." He added: "With the Defender, there's no messing. People like it as it is—tough and simple. The Freelander is an opportunity to move the whole Land Rover thinking on. We've done it before with the Range Rover. It had to be completely contemporary."

Land Rover cues McGovern deemed as essential to the Freelander were the

The five-door wagon and two-door hardtop Freelanders, below, were revealed at the 1997 Frankfurt Motor Show. Recent styling revisions have included new headlights and frontal treatment, opposite.

"clamshell" hood that makes engine access unfettered, the castellations on the leading edges of the hood top that make the vehicle easy to place on the road and in tight corners, and the equal glass-to-bodywork relationship that makes Land Rovers—usually taller than other cars—still look balanced. McGovern also considered the wheels, the prominence of the door hinges, and the length by which the body "overhangs" the vehicle's wheelbase.

Overall, the five-door station wagon works better than the rather fussily resolved three-door, with its slopeback metalwork and addition of a hood or a hardtop to complete its profile. On both cars, however, there is a giving in to large, ugly plastic moldings that definitely were not part of any previous Land Rover's makeup. They are no doubt intended for all the supermarket parking-lot blockades the car is

likely to encounter accidentally but, perhaps, it was one element that was changed for the better in 2003 when the Freelander received the interlinked-circle headlight clusters and body-colored bumpers that brought it into line with the Range Rover and latest Discovery. The industry expects that an all-new model will seek to push the Freelander ever closer in style to its larger brothers.

Final styling proposals for the most controversial Land Rover so far are shown opposite top. Designer Gerry McGovern worked hard to retain brand design cues, opposite bottom. The two-door Freelander's style was certainly characterful, if a little fussy, right and below.

BMW X3/X5

It may be slipping into ancient history now, but it's a fact: from 1994 until 2000, BMW possessed a legendary name in the history of four-wheel drive, off-roading, and ultimately SUVs—Land Rover. And yet despite having access to the decades of in-the-field experience Land Rover held in these areas, BMW studiously avoided any cross-pollination between its British subsidiary and the design mothership in Munich. The BMW X5 SUV was developed in total isolation from Land Rover, which, bearing in mind that the X5 was launched in 1999, must raise eyebrows about BMW's commitment in the first place to what its executives later referred to as "the English patient."

Or maybe it was just that BMW—accurately—recognized the future for SUVs as being one in which the focus needed to be on strong on-road performance with merely visual overtones of ruggedness, and that there was little Land Rover could tell it about this emerging automotive discipline.

The X5 was also a bridgehead for US expansion, to be built in BMW's new Spartanburg plant in South Carolina, and destined primarily to satisfy American drivers' ambitions. Here, then, was another area in which Land Rover had little to offer.

The X5 is a successful melding of BMW's trademark design sparingness with an aggressive high-riding stance. It looks like, and is, a BMW Touring wagon pumped up to SUV proportions with lines that are at once quite conservative in detail but assertive in attitude. The steroids seem to have worked around the wheelarches and lower doors, where the whole car appears flared out around fat alloy wheels and low-profile tires. The shallow BMW "twin kidney" grille and narrow headlights hint at the gritty determination that all BMWs exude to force their way through the motoring landscape, while a strong indented waistline set up on the front fenders runs along the car's flanks and wraps around its tailgate to delineate the prosperous occupants visible in the glasshouse from the

From every angle, the BMW X5 embraces visual aggression with glee, while also providing a decidedly carlike upper section to draw in traditional BMW sedan buyers.

RY51 UMH

grubby business of wheeled propulsion going on below.

It's a well resolved design, albeit one that, due to the strength of BMW's somewhat self-centered brand message, defines an SUV that divides the world into advocates and opponents. Notably, when BMW applied its strategy of the same car in different sizes to its "X" series "Sports Activity Vehicle" sub-brand by bringing out a smaller model, the 3 Series-based X3, it possessed a toned-down styling "thrust"; as a more affordable entrée to BMW ownership, it makes a rather milder statement.

The X3 also adopts BMW's recent design language, with the interplay of concave and convex surfaces for the "flame surfacing" effect pioneered by BMW design chief Chris Bangle on the CS1 concept car in 2001. There is the reinterpretation of BMW's classic "Hofmeister kick" (a detail named for Wilhelm Hofmeister, BMW's first-ever stylist) in the rear side window, and the double-kidney grille is a centerpiece of a neatly rounded frontal countenance. The wheelarches bulge and the roofline slowly drops to the rear for some additional dynamic character.

Neither the X5 nor the X3, despite their design urgency, puts up an especially gruff performance in off-road duties, and the low ground clearance of the X3 in particular militates against heavy off-road use. Yet for BMW fanciers caught on the cusp of the SUV trend, these two cars press all the right buttons.

The BMW X3 on these pages is a softer, more accessible take on the midsize SUV concept, adapting its interplay of convex and concave shapes from other models in the range.

Audi allroad · Renault Megane Scenic 4x4

A vehicle with a separate chassis is much easier and cheaper to redesign than an "all-in-one" monocoque. You can't unpick a unit-construction body without losing the structure's innate strength—and putting that back in is near-impossible. However, the majority of modern cars have a surprising modularity to their outer panels—that is, the nose, front fenders, hood, tailgate, or trunk, and rear bumper/valance section. Altering any or all of these panels can be done without disturbing the main architecture of the car beneath. In theory, the same goes for the surface profile of the doors, although this is rarely done during the life cycle of a model.

All of this means that most cars can, and do, receive midterm makeovers to see them through a life cycle during which they can suddenly face new rivals. And it also means that spin-off variants can be given a distinctive new look for a fraction of the cost of an entirely new vehicle. This trick allowed two European makes with no SUV traditions to draw on to enter the fray in 2000 and snatch a piece of the action from industry leaders such as Land Rover and BMW.

The Audi allroad quattro (Audi likes using lowercase letters to denote its variants) is claimed by the company to be "purpose-designed for the nascent 'allroader' segment in the USA," but that doesn't tell the whole story. Its body structure is that of the Audi A6 Avant, but a significantly raised ride height and larger wheels elevate the car to a midsize between a normal station wagon and a full-size SUV such as a BMW X5. However, Audi is cautious in explaining the car's role as being "able to cope with even the poorest of roads and weather conditions." There is no mention of polar expeditions or farmland tasks.

Ingenious application of black plastic panel sections and aluminum-finish highlights, together with a suitably raised ride height, helped Audi create a "halfway-house" SUV out of its A6 Avant model; light off-road capability is the impression, and the reality, for this car.

Along the "cutline" between the grille and bumper, the allroad features reprofiled bumpers in a matt-finish, scratch-proof dark gray plastic, together with a similar treatment at the rear. A ribbed shiny metal section pokes out at either end of the car; Audi calls it a "protective underdrive device," which is really a fancy name for a drivetrain shield that runs the entire length of the car's underside.

To the side profile, prominent semicircular black plastic flares are attached to the standard A6 wheelarches for protection from stone chips, while bright-finish, bulging aluminum-style strips along the bottom of the doors draw the eye to the reassuringly large gap between the base of the metalwork and the ground below.

While the allroad is a convincing amalgam of sleek road car and upright 4x4, Renault's Scenic RX4 uses similar methodology for a completely different aesthetic. The Megane Scenic was the pioneering compact multi-purpose vehicle (MPV) in 1996, an acclaimed design of tall-bodied, five-seater family wagon created under the eye of Renault design guru Patrick le Quément, with Anne Asensio working on the concept and Anthony Grade executing the brilliantly versatile interior. Appropriately, it was voted European Car of the Year in 1997.

The Scenic has an overwhelmingly ovular profile, making it almost a "one-box" design with a steeply raked hood and an extreme curve to the side window line. Raising this car to give it rough terrain capability meant putting the egg on stilts, lifting an already vertically commodious vehicle to near-Jeep Grand Cherokee heights, but Renault went to further stylistic lengths to differentiate the car from its more prosaic "road" version.

Again using the "cutline" between bumper and grille, a pugnacious new nose section was attached, incorporating protruding overriders, round and sunken spotlights, and the shiny edge of the sump guard. At the back, the treatment was even more radical: using the "cutline" where the bodywork matched the lift-up tailgate of the original Scenic, a new two-piece rear opening was fitted. The top half is a lift-up glass tailgate, but the bottom is a swing-out door, with its hinges on the outside and a recess cut into the black plastic bumper to accommodate its opening, carrying the spare wheel in a body-colored cover.

To drive behind the Scenic is to follow a vehicle that seems to be carrying a shiny, upended dustbin. But with a pseudo-SUV like this, conventional design thinking is put to one side—and that has to be more interesting.

The ovular basic form of the Megane Scenic was given a distinctive work over by Renault's design team, led by Patrick le Quément, including the substitution of a versatile split tailgate design to put maximum emphasis on the car's active lifestyle bent.

Pontiac Aztek

"**W**ith Aztek, Pontiac has produced a love-it-or-hate-it vehicle." That is what the old-established division of General Motors itself says of its 2001 debutante in the burgeoning "crossover" SUV market, and many commentators have tended to go for the latter verdict. The Aztek is a regular on "ugliest car" lists from outspoken car critics, and indeed its lines could hardly be described as sleek and certainly not sensual.

The Aztek's emergence from a company that rarely elects to court controversy in design terms—General Motors is far too serious an enterprise for that—is symptomatic of the crowded and copycat nature of the American market. With an explosion of SUV models at the end of the century, the genre turned almost overnight from niche to mainstream. The problem was that the vast majority of offerings

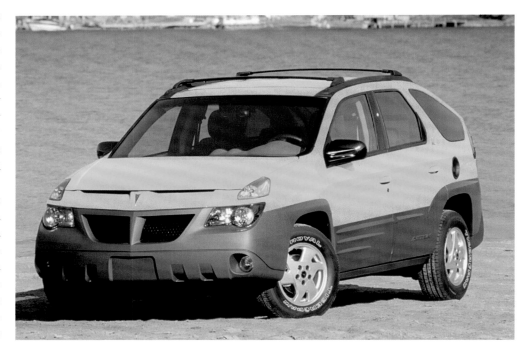

To own a Pontiac Aztek, quite probably, is to love it, especially with such novel options as a camping pack, opposite bottom, but its ugly-for-a-good-reason looks are certainly not to the taste of many traditional sedan owners.

tended to be either derivative of what had slowly evolved over fifty years (that is, the vehicles featured in this book) or else so bland and visually "safe" that their message could not be heard over the hearty chorus of the US establishment.

Pontiac set out to change all that with the Aztek. Its styling, in which straight lines fight furiously for attention, was previewed in a yellow-and-gray 1999 concept vehicle of the same name, but the 2001 production car was rather different in character. The concept had a triangulated pugnaciousness to it, with its pointed prow setting up the whole car's design from a frontal centerpoint. The hood was prominent, with a double-deck, stacked air intake, and the side windows dropped below

the hood level to meet a waistline that rose toward the rear end. A slope-back roof aft of the forward-slanting C-pillars gave the impression, thanks to the split in the paint colors, of a tacked-on rear awning.

In the production vehicle, this conflict was junked in favor of a design hybrid with simply a corresponding profile. The upper part of the Aztek resembles a five-door hatchback sedan body mass, complete with a vertical glazed tail panel between its high-mounted rear lights, which has been parachuted on to the rugged lower contours of a military vehicle, all molded plastic in an uneasy mix of jagged edges and smooth tapers. It is at the front that the showroom Aztek has retained the strongest link with its concept forerunner, with its additional

lateral air intake in the leading edge of the hood and the alert-looking, high-mounted, triangular indicator lenses.

Despite offering various interesting outdoor-pursuit option kits, such as a camping pack to turn the vehicle into a cramped mobile home, the Aztek came at first with front-wheel drive only. Although four-wheel drive was subsequently offered, this was a hint toward the intended Aztek buyer—American families with an active bent but no real use for off-road

On the Aztek, a multitude of straight lines do visual battle for attention; the upper section of the car resembles a five-door hatchback, while the lower portion exudes amphibious military truck.

capability. The marketing subheading was "Sport Recreation Vehicle." The Aztek is intended as a compromise between sports sedan, sport utility vehicle, and minivan but, unlike recent offerings from rivals, the utilitarian design element—rather than the sporty one—is the strongest. It's the "ugly for a good reason" school of thought: one that, for once, is counter-aspirational and pro-practical, evinced by the emphasis on interior versatility with such features as configurable seating patterns, two optional storage packages, a fold-down tailgate, and a standard console cooler that holds twelve beverage cans. So whatever observers or peers may think, to own an Aztek is probably to appreciate it; this works in other sectors, notably the multipurpose vehicle one, but it is pretty daring in an area like SUVs, where, for most people, image is everything.

Hyundai Santa Fe/Tucson

South Korea's first, biggest, and most successful carmaker came to the SUV market very cautiously, entering it in the early 1990s with a license-built version of the first Mitsubishi Pajero, rather amusingly sold as the Galloper. In January 2000, however, when Hyundai unveiled the Santa Fe at the Detroit Auto Show, it looked to be merely the latest in a long line of arresting show cars that were unlikely to be seen or heard of again, with its swoopy contours, copper paintwork, and gleaming chrome wheels. Essentially it was a toned-down version of a similar vehicle shown the year before. But then Hyundai revealed that this was the almost-finished prototype of its actual SUV—and the wry grins vanished.

The Santa Fe now on sale is amazingly true to that show car. It has a bulbous, muscular feel to all the metalwork below the waistline, with the fenders and hood seemingly straining at their seams to restrain the car's off-road energy. The snub-nosed grille suggests eagerness, while the rounded corners of the bumper sections, together with large circular spotlamps buried in nacelles below the headlamps, hint at further intent. Meanwhile, on top, a glasshouse of typical family wagon proportions gives the Santa Fe its approachable scale; it's almost as if the car's cabin has been "cut-and-shut" in the good old US customizing tradition.

Indeed, there is American influence throughout the Santa Fe, and not just in its name.

The guiding light behind this radical design was thirty-six-year-old Derek Sancer, the first American designer Hyundai had employed at its Fountain Valley Design Center in California, where the Santa Fe was developed in its entirety in stiff competition with Hyundai facilities in Frankfurt, Germany, and Namyang, South Korea. Sancer explained:

We looked at the competition and saw their advantages and disadvantages. We wanted to innovate but do it with style and at a lower cost. I was big on motorcycles and wanted to keep the same philosophy going. We didn't design it to be market-specific; if it looks good it will look good in any country.

The rounded, sculptural forms of the Hyundai Santa Fe were developed not in South Korea but in sun-kissed California, where designers sought to make the car "an intriguing proposition from the start."

Anyway, customer clinics tend to frown on a bold design and stick with what they know. The Santa Fe had to be an intriguing proposition from the start. We are delighted at the public response, which has improved the overall image of Hyundai and attracted many first-time buyers. It's quite an achievement to change the perception of a brand.

An emboldened Hyundai in 2004 launched a smaller SUV alternative to the Santa Fe, the Tucson. Proof that the base engineering of such cars has come a very long way since the 1940s and 50s is that this car shares the platform of the low-slung Hyundai Coupé. From the front, the affinity to the Santa Fe is clear, but the side profile is razor-edged in contrast, with a snug glasshouse as befits what is, essentially, a high-riding family hatchback that comes with four driven wheels. With the Santa Fe cleaving open the SUV market for Hyundai in recent years, it's pretty sure to find ready appreciation.

Hyundai extended its reach downward into the compact SUV arena with the 2004 Tucson, shown opposite and right, aiming the car at buyers needing an accessible entrée to SUVs. The 2000 Detroit show car, above, rapidly went on sale as the Santa Fe.

Dodge Durango

Bob Lutz is a legendary figure in the US automotive industry, a self-professed "car guy" who has had influential spells at each of the "Big Three": Ford, Chrysler, and today, as chairman, General Motors. His influence at Chrysler can be witnessed in such memorable cars as the Dodge Viper and the Plymouth Prowler, strongly "retro" speciality models that paved the way for the Chrysler PT Cruiser, a family car disguised as a homage to 1950s hot-rodding for the dad who never wants to feel old. But the most commercially significant launch under Lutz's reign was the Dodge Ram pickup, and it is this vehicle that lent its strong, upfront, and unapologetically American character to the Dodge Durango.

The Ram made its debut in 1994. It was Chrysler's first all-new full-size pickup in twenty-two years, and it was intended to inject some excitement into what had become an uninspiring sector (albeit a highly profitable one for GM and Ford). Lutz encouraged Chrysler/Dodge designers to give the Ram the bullish character found in typical US articulated truck cabs like Kenworths and Peterbilts, which were familiar for their massive, bluff nose treatments that had become chrome-laden icons of highways across the USA.

Like a Peterbilt, then, the Ram sported a prominent powerhouse of a hood fronted by a mesh-backed, heavily chrome-surrounded radiator grille. The hood did not have to work hard to suggest the huge horsepower offered by what it enclosed on front, sides, and top—the world's first V10 production engine, and the most powerful unit ever fitted to a US pickup. On either side of this colossal snout, low-set headlamps established lower-level fenders that were pulled back until they bled away to nothing in the door panels. The hood shape, meanwhile, flared out to meet the bases of the A-pillars and then formed the waistline that led back into the edge of the pickup loading bay.

The Ram was certainly a headline grabber, and it was judged such a success with American consumers that the style was aped for Dodge's smaller pickup line, the Dakota, launched in 1997. A smaller scale gave the style less impact but the general Dodge "trademark" look translated well. A year later the Durango was launched, using the Dakota as a mechanical base—which meant, of course, a heavy separate

The Dodge Durango, below and opposite bottom, used the Dodge Dakota basis as a shortcut to join the modern SUV generation. The Dodge Durango "Dude," opposite top, demonstrates the lean-and-mean image portrayed by Dodge's contemporary truck range.

chassis, making this a resolutely old-school SUV in stark contrast to, say, the "Uniframe" Jeep Grand Cherokee (although there was something of that Jeep's profile to the Durango's rear fenders). However, after the visual excitement that the frontal aspect establishes, the rest of the vehicle is slightly underwhelming. With the huge sales numbers involved when a company decides to take on the Ford Explorer and the Chevrolet Tahoe, design adventurousness is necessarily restricted. The Durango was striking—perhaps the epitome of traditional US SUV design at the time—but, to its core market, anything but alienating. Yet despite the Lutz touch, the Durango, with its massive weight and power, and hefty construction, has the aura of being among the last of a slowly dying breed.

The Dodge Dakota, opposite top, shows its family resemblance to the Durango. The Durango's interior is shown opposite bottom. The vehicle is handsome in an all-American way, right. The original 1994 Ram pickup, below, proved a very influential vehicle.

Lincoln Navigator - Cadillac Escalade/Cadillac SRX

Ownership of an upscale car brand in the first decade of the twenty-first century puts the proprietor under an obligation that would have been unthinkable twenty years ago: you've got to have a sport utility vehicle in your lineup almost no matter what your heritage represents. Once, the Range Rover was the lonely weirdo of the luxury SUV world, but now even race-bred brands like Jaguar—which stood back loftily as the segment mushroomed—suffer through not having an equivalent offering to Lexus, Mercedes-Benz, BMW, and Jeep.

US giants Ford and General Motors knew there was an urgent need for product-planning action in the late 1990s, but were caught on the horns of a dilemma. Respective Lincoln and Cadillac offerings needed to be large and imposing to meet customer expectations of these premium brands, and yet to develop models from scratch for such niche markets was economically unviable. Inevitably, the two companies had to fall back on the methodology they have both adopted time and again: emblem engineering. If the product does not exist then create it from what you already make and sprinkle in the right marketing stardust to achieve your aims.

In a way, this is an excellent challenge for designers, and the studios tried hard to give the so-called "full-size" Ford Expedition a Lincoln-like character with a mild reworking of the front panels, a concentration on unique appliqué trim, wheels and emblem, and a plush interior to create the 1998 Lincoln Navigator. Stung into immediate retaliation, Cadillac took the Chevrolet/GMC Suburban and effected a similar transformation to create the 1999 Cadillac Escalade.

Clumsy or handsome—make of these cars' heavy chrome visages and gratuitous interior opulence what you will, they have satisfied customers ranging from the ghetto-fabulous to the elderly rancher, taking in company executives and Middle Eastern minor royalty along the way. Both the Navigator and the Escalade have been welcome contributors to the coffers of their manufacturers, with the Lincoln Navigator sometimes talked of as one of

The Lincoln Navigator has one of the most prominent chrome grilles found anywhere in the car industry, but underneath the Detroit glitz this is still a Ford Expedition.

Ford's most profitable products at margins of some $25,000; this is great news for two companies that constantly weather good and bad news in their global reaches.

But the reason the Navigator and Escalade make so much money is also the very reason they are, really, design-bankrupt. They cost virtually nothing to develop, use old-fashioned existing technology (both ride on substantial separate chassis frames and derive their power from thirsty V8 engines), and have architecture carried over from other, existing vehicles. There was a limit to what any designer could achieve with this straitjacket on, and neither the Navigator nor the Escalade do their brands any favors in terms of design integrity—the very thing, ironically, that holds them back against progressive nameplates such as the famous German duo of BMW and Mercedes-Benz.

The Cadillac SRX, however, shows some more individualistic Cadillac thinking. It is a high-riding station wagon with an impressive frontal appearance given added height by vertical stacks of headlights at each corner, a strong, shapely side profile, and full-fat proportions. It clearly reflects Cadillac's newly

defined "design language" pioneered by the Evoq roadster concept in 1999; simply, structural and boxy proportions using chiseled forms with straight feature lines. The aim is to make it eye-catching opposite its softer-looking rivals like the Infiniti FX45—to offer something that is staunchly and immediately American in appearance. Unlike the curvaceous Infiniti, the SRX's rear side glass and tailgate are visually disjointed along the waistline from the main seating area, suggesting that there is a separate and spacious luggage area. The interior, however, is a dull, molded sea of gray, barely enlivened by dark polished wood and cream leather. Once again, the FX45 has a more special, "tailored" ambience.

GM vice president Harry Pearce, interviewed in 2000 about soaring sales of SUVs, said: "If pigs are big and popular, I guess we'll make pigs." This is fine from the corporate standpoint of keeping shareholders happy, but the Navigator and Escalade did not give their makers a head start in a sector that has become design-conscious almost overnight. Hopefully, they will be remembered as a compromised start, and the SRX a promising second step.

The Escalade, opposite, may be a dinosaur in the Detroit tradition, but the SRX, this page, proves that US companies can make a mark on the crossover SUV world.

Lexus RX300

With the launch of the Mercedes-Benz M-Class in 1997, the SUV format moved into the "premium" make arena that the Range Rover, until that point, had had pretty much to itself. In short, premium makes comprise the German duo of BMW and Mercedes-Benz, Britain's Jaguar, Bentley, and Rolls-Royce, Japan's Lexus (Toyota) and Infiniti (Nissan), and Cadillac (GM) and Lincoln (Ford) from the USA. They all make four-door sedans that fulfill their roles as well as any other but, for reasons of history, applied technology, contrivance, and marketing, are able to be sold at a massive margin. Mercedes-Benz is the world leader at this, and whatever it does is likely to be quickly copied by its rivals.

Lexus was thus jolted into action in 1998 to create instantly a Lexus off-roader. The simple expedient was equipping and re-branding a Toyota Land Cruiser as the Lexus LX470. It was an extremely unconvincing move, but Toyota had a more appropriate product in its Harrier SUV, which had been a big pull at the 1997 Tokyo Motor Show. Very little effort was needed or involved in tidying up the Harrier's fussy Japanese edges to create the Lexus RX300, ready to take on the SUV establishment in the USA and Europe, while the Harrier itself remained a product for predominantly Japanese consumption only.

Initial impressions of the RX300 are of a smooth-looking executive car with plenty of distance between the cabin and ground level and with an additional glazed station-wagon section seemingly grafted on to its back end;

Few buyers of the original RX300, below, realized that the car had first seen the light as the Japan-only Toyota Harrier, opposite bottom. The 2003 replacement, opposite top, was aerodynamically refined in the same wind tunnel as Japan's Bullet Train.

the substantial, steeply raked C-pillar suggests that there is a "sedan" version even though there is not. Low-profile tires on large alloy wheels indicate that RX300 owners are more concerned with keeping their cars looking shiny than tackling mountain tracks, while gigantic door mirrors suggest plenty of help for those tricky urban driving maneuvers. Substantial, squared-off, wheelarch bulges, however, add some surface machismo to an overall quite benign shape.

The only drawback for the RX300, in some ways, was its station-wagon aesthetic, but that was remedied in 2003 by a new RX300, which was turned into a five-door hatchback coupé along similar, if slightly chunkier, lines. A shallow glasshouse twinned with a high waistline and a horizontal door molding, a third of the way up the panels, link the front and rear wheelarch bulges, nonetheless creating a shape that is much more racy than anything in the SUV line so far from archrival Mercedes-Benz.

The shovel-like nose treatment with a typically Lexus vertically latticed grille is combined with modern, clear glass lamps at front and rear, and large 17-in. (432-mm) six-spoke or 18-in. (457-mm) five-spoke alloy wheels to give the car an imposing image. It is highly unusual for the designer of a Japanese car to be openly credited—its manufacturers like to present their wares as team efforts—but in this case the project's chief designer has been revealed as Takumi Ichikawa. It is said to be his passion for the dynamism of aeronautical shapes that provided the inspiration for the RX300 exterior design, as evinced by the aircraft-inspired, rising belt line to the rear—to express the speed and stance of a jet fighter aircraft. The tailgate design, meanwhile, features an integral rear spoiler that aids aerodynamic efficiency and stability and helps keep the rear window clean. It is highly appropriate, then, that the RX300 has been tested in the same wind tunnel in Japan that was used to refine aerodynamically the Shinkansen "Bullet Train." The tunnel's very low background noise allowed Lexus to cut wind noise by refining the position of the A-pillars and parked windshield wipers, at the same time as achieving a drag coefficient of 0.34. That class-

leading figure was attained by something that cannot be seen on the outside of the RX300—extremely effective undercar streamlining, and an electronic system that lowers the car by $\frac{5}{16}$ in. (7.5 mm) at speed to make it hug the ground even more closely. It is the world's most aerodynamic SUV but, thanks to short overhangs, it can still tackle reasonably demanding gradients.

The original RX300, right, has helped propel Lexus to market-leading customer satisfaction in the USA. The images below and opposite contrast the tail treatment of the two RX300 series, showing the more "carlike" direction that Lexus has opted for.

Volvo XC90

A graduate of the Royal College of Art in London, Briton Peter Horbury is responsible for the successful look of the Volvo XC90. He began work as Volvo's design director in 1991 (today he is in charge of design at Ford in Detroit), and almost immediately got down to pinpointing what exactly it is, in design terms, that characterizes the make's cars. He then set about encapsulating it in a concept sedan car called the Volvo ECC.

"I actually hate 'retro'; that's not what we're about," Horbury said in a 1999 interview, discussing the ECC, with the author. He continued:

But the positive arc from the front lamp to the back one was there since the Volvo PV444 of 1947. Then there was the shoulder that didn't "fall away" immediately from the bottom of the side windows. It's solid, strong, a flattop shoulder that came from the 140 and 240. On top was what we call the "Volvo bridge"— three side windows with a dogleg shape at the back. The 400, 800, and 900 series—they all had that. It was the basic architecture of a Volvo in a very new way. I felt we'd managed almost a subconscious recognition. Unlike previous Volvos, though, we didn't want the car's safety to be in-your-face.

In the subsequent Volvo production cars, such as the S80, this tightly focused "Volvoness," as Horbury described it, was made real. Intriguingly, the description of the ECC above would also perfectly match the XC90, which made its debut at the Detroit Auto Show in 2002, long anticipated as Volvo's first-ever SUV.

Retro the XC90 certainly wasn't, although its forward-jutting snout and strong, solid lines would not have looked out of place on a 1950s railway locomotive. In side profile, it shares the BMW X5's muscular stance but otherwise it is all Volvo, from the V-shaped hood to the characteristic taillamps that seem to "plug" the end of that broad, beamlike shoulder. The passenger compartment on the XC90 goes for a cab-forward proportion so Volvo could make the car, at a push, a seven-seater SUV within its 16-ft. (4.8-m) length; to emphasize this the rear

The XC90 is probably the most accomplished-looking Volvo of all time, rolling traditional brand values into the SUV genre with extraordinary success for a make with no previous off-road offering.

doors are, unusually, very slightly larger than the front ones. The tailgate has a sporty angle for a truncated roofline that implies purposefulness.

"Masculine but not macho; muscular but not aggressive," is how Horbury described the car: "Nobody should be in any doubt that this is a modern Volvo. Everyone rides in Business Class in the Volvo XC90, nobody travels economy class. It is true that the third row of seats isn't built for full-size adults, but a modern family rarely needs room for seven grown-ups in its car anyway."

The XC90 makes you wonder why Volvo did not produce this car much sooner, so well does it mesh with the make's brand values and existing product range. The answer, of course, is economies of scale: Volvo could never have developed the XC90 unless it had the resources of its new parent company, Ford, which took over in 2000, to draw on for ready-made four-wheel drive components. Indeed, demand for the XC90 was so instant and strong that it took

the company by surprise as it struggled to meet a cascade of orders. In 2004, it became Volvo's top-selling model globally.

However, the very accessibility of the Volvo brand ethos has helped make the XC90, along with the BMW X5 and Porsche Cayenne, among the most popular targets for resentment from non-SUV-driving urbanites in Europe, who feel with some justification that a car of this size is not necessary for taking children to school and transporting an expensively attired parent with no more cargo than two bags of groceries. It is the small, and possibly rather sour, price that Volvo pays for defining the modern European SUV so skillfully.

This Volvo Adventure Concept Car, opposite, shown in 2001, proved an accurate pointer to the style of the impending XC90. The XC90 has terrific off-road ability, this page, to match its undoubted prestige in the "school run" parade.

Hummer H1

As a feeder of off-road fantasies, the Hummer H1 is unrivaled. Its military might means it literally rides roughshod over the rules that govern most regular production cars, but its overtly combative appearance exerts as much pull on grown-up schoolboys with fantasy war records as it does on genuine defense clients. The Hummer is warfare on wheels, and that holds a strong attraction for all sorts of minds. Its manufacturer, AM General Corporation, was acquired by General Motors in 2000 in an astute move to cash in on this attraction by exploiting "Hummer" as a true brand, and two years later the Hummer H2 emerged as a pastiche of the original, which now became the H1. The H2 was much smaller, of course, and while it is an extremely competent off-roader, its militaristic outward appearance makes it a pale, cowardly shadow of the huge original.

The parallels between the H1 and the original Willys Jeep are obvious. The vehicle was never styled at all, but rather mapped out to fulfill a range of extremely demanding US Army requirements to create the ultimate in go-anywhere vehicles that could be specified in several variations and could resist just about anything thrown at it. It did not have to be that fast; just unstoppable.

The underpinnings called for a ladder-frame separate chassis so the vehicle could be configured in a variety of ways, from troop carrier to minitank to ambulance, and independent suspension by wishbones and coil springs for the ultimate in ground clearance combined with wheel articulation. The bodywork, often to be armor-plated, would then follow each function with no concession to anything except sheer purpose. AM General and US Army chiefs set to with their geometry sets to create the

ultimate in antistyling, making no attempt to disguise rivets, bracing, or hinges, and leaving only the tires with any compound curves.

The link to Jeep was fundamental because AM General had been split off from American Motors in 1983 and was, in fact, the Indiana-based division that had made military Jeeps. The 1979 blueprint for the vehicle referred to it as the High Mobility Multi-Purpose Wheeled Vehicle, and within fifteen months the design had been turned into working prototypes for appraisal. Fully satisfied that it was just what it

Off-road vehicle? The Hummer almost defines the term, and the two-door pickup edition, below as an open-air troop carrier and opposite bottom, sees the H1 in its most basic form. The four-door "sedan," opposite top, is 14 in. (356 mm) wider than the widest Chevrolet sedan.

needed, the US Army placed a $1.2 billion order for 55,000 "HMMWVs" or "Humvees" in 1983. As the vehicles began to enter service in the late 1980s, they gained the more pronounceable "Hummer" nickname from troops.

The 1991 Gulf War was the Hummer's launch advertising campaign as far as the public was concerned, as the 7-liter giants were witnessed on television screens worldwide liberating Kuwait from Iraqi invasion. Desire rose from conflict and, in 1992, a "civilian" model of what had become the Hummer M998 was introduced. It had a 6.2-liter diesel V8 as standard, but a detuned Chevrolet Corvette gas V8 was offered in 1995. It cost up to $45,000 and came in four body configurations, including a four-door soft-top, and with items not found on army models, such as keyed ignition and even seatbelts. One thing customers could order,

however, was Hummer's automatic tire deflation and inflation system to provide ideal pressures depending on the terrain conditions. AM General sold around one thousand nonmilitary Hummers a year, and total Hummer production settled down to a steady 3500 annually.

What set the vehicle apart even from the biggest, toughest American SUVs was that it was designed specifically for off-road driving. At 14 in. (35.5 cm) wider even than the widest Chevrolet sedan, conducting this trucklike monster along the highway would be tricky work for all but the most skilled drivers. And that, of course, would be the challenge to most buyers. But General Motors was able to sanitize the ultraraw Hummer image for a wider audience in the H2, while owning a valuable franchise in military vehicles that, as long as conflict in the Middle East and elsewhere

continues, is bound to lead to plenty of repeat orders. Ford and DaimlerChrysler must be kicking themselves for missing this one-shot acquisition opportunity.

The Hummer H1, below and opposite top in four-door hard- and soft-top versions, tends to suit larger-than-life characters or those who harbor fantasies about their military prowess. The vehicle has demonstrated its prowess in off-road events, opposite bottom, as if it needed to prove anything after its role in Kuwait's 1991 liberation.

Porsche Cayenne · Volkswagen Touareg

The Porsche Cayenne is, perhaps, the most contentious of all SUVs so far because, a few years ago, it would have seemed the least likely. Porsche, the German make with a heritage unsullied by ill-advised diversifications and made glorious by its unbroken duo of leading sports car design and global motor sport supremacy, joined the sport utility stampede in October 2002 with a car that, in shape and concept, was diametrically opposed to anything it had previously done.

However, in the automotive industry, times change, and they change for good. Jaguar chief designer Ian Callum recently told the author, for instance, that there would never be another car like the classic Jaguar E-type, and then proceeded to explain the reasons why—a complex matrix of regulations designed to protect both pedestrians and car occupants from injury in a variety of collisions. The upshot of this is that mass-produced, front-engined,

The Cayenne's multifaceted personality is well illustrated in these images. The initial consternation of Porsche traditionalists has been silenced by huge sales.

ground-hugging sports cars will be almost impossible to create around a "soft zone" between the hood and the top of the engine to cushion a pedestrian unlucky enough to be struck by the car.

So what, you may say: Porsche sports cars like the Boxster and the 911 have their engines at the back. This is true, but just about everyone who can indulge in a premium-priced Porsche is already doing so. The only way for a publicly quoted Porsche to expand its activities, and boost its shareholder dividends, is to find something else to build.

Dull though this industry strategy may sound, it is the sort of thing that informed the decision to proceed with the Cayenne. Fortunately for matters of both heritage and also viability, Porsche found an excellent ally in Volkswagen, a fellow German brand in

desperate need of an "in" to the hot SUV sector. This is the reason why the two companies made such perfect partners in the collaboration that created both the Cayenne and the Volkswagen Touareg, for this pair are the same car interpreted in individual ways.

For once, the Volkswagen is the slicker design. It does nothing so much as take the benignly confident look of the Golf and Passat and translate it to SUV proportions. Seen in isolation and with nothing to give it scale, it would be hard to prove the Touareg was not simply a spacious family hatchback. The non-aggressive, circular wheelarches, the failsafe size of the light clusters, the bulging, organic-looking side profile that manages to look sleek without the aid of horizontal swage lines—it is that classic Volkswagen simplicity, refined by design chief Hartmut Warkuss, that treads the expert line between looking smart yet feeling inclusive.

In the Cayenne, we find an identical center section—the door panels and glass are the same, as dictated by the platform below, and by financial logic—but the front and rear ends are resolved very differently. And, to many, it is an unhappy match of Porsche 911 detailing in the headlights and the fit of the nose section/bumper to the front fenders, with a distinctly un-Porsche blocky clumsiness to the heavily executed rear end. The more sharklike frontal aspect (compared with the Touareg) accentuates the less harmonious tail section even further, although the curved-round finish to the window line does its best to disguise the station-wagon design dynamic that the Touareg so comfortably embraces.

Porsche, of course, can always claim that a Cayenne would never be a replacement for one of its sports cars, rather a complementary motoring possession for the well-heeled Porsche devotee; a Volkswagen buyer may well be ordering a Touareg as an alternative to a Phaeton limousine, a Passat sedan, or a Sharan MPV. A Cayenne Turbo has genuine, fire-breathing Porsche V8 power, while diesels, albeit the world's most powerful, are strictly the province of VW. But the design debate will rage on until Porsche is forced by sheer volume of

white-hot rivalry—everything from the next-generation Jeep Grand Cherokee and Range Rover to the effortless style confidence of the Infiniti FX45—to declare its next SUV hand. Meanwhile, for many people, the elegant Volkswagen has the quietly confident upper hand in the premium SUV arena.

The Volkswagen Touareg, shown right, below, and opposite bottom, is a rather more sober design than the Cayenne. The AAC concept, opposite top, explores new avenues down which Touareg-based cars could carry the VW name.

Nissan was a part of the SUV scene from the outset thanks to its venerable Patrol series, but it would have taken a brave forecaster to predict that the once-dowdy Japanese company would hold design leadership in the field at the dawn of the twenty-first century. Arguably, however, it's in this exalted position that Nissan now finds itself with this handsome pair of vehicles.

All thoughts of creating vehicles to trudge their way through farmyard mud or battlefield sand are in the past. The 2002 Murano was conceived from the outset as the pinnacle of crossover—a high-riding, front-wheel drive family car with a high-performance gas engine (no commerce-friendly diesel is offered) and a continuously variable automatic transmission that can nonetheless employ its high ground clearance (partly thanks to enormous 18-in./457-mm alloy wheels) and automatically activated four-wheel drive mode to ride

proudly and securely over slush, boggy ground, or icy, cobbled streets.

The Murano's styling is distinctively laid-back. Its most unusual features are its steeply rising window lines aft of the rear doors, and a razor-edged rear fender profile that curves down markedly at the heavy-looking, truncated back of the car in harmony with the wheelarch and the profile of the huge rear light clusters. The slatted chrome grille cover, with seductively narrow headlights echoing Nissan's 350Z sports cars, has a wedge-shaped profile that makes most of the Murano's potential rivals look like motorized battleships. Short front and rear overhangs plant the car to the road like an oversize Hot Wheels toy.

The Murano ethos is coastal American, as the car was created at Nissan's Californian design studio. Heading its design team was Taiji Toyota. The company wanted something that sat on top of the line dividing hardcore 4x4s as

evinced by the Nissan Patrol, conventional family cars like the Nissan Primera, and sports cars like the 350Z, using Nissan's FFL (for Front engine, Front drive, Large) platform.

"Murano is a cool fusion between a conventional sedan and a true SUV," said Mr Toyota, "a genuine crossover. But Murano is also a symbolic car: dynamic, sporty, robust, and secure. It's a very progressive design, a car with a good stance that makes a great impression the moment you first see it. It is a very different-looking car yet it is clearly a Nissan." This is true in its unusual, triangulated rear window, a feature seen before on Nissan concepts like the Qashqai and the Tone.

Nissan has formulated another model offering a slightly remixed cocktail of sport and utility (and its FM platform, shared with the 350Z), selling it as the Infiniti FX45 exclusively in the USA. The highly confident proportions recall those of a close-coupled station wagon,

The Murano is a masterful example of crossover thinking in the SUV sector, with little of the startling style of early design sketches, opposite, lost in the transition to production car status. The crude, early Nissan Patrol now seems a distant memory.

yet with an arched, executive carlike window line and a roof the leading edge of which drifts gently down over the rear quarterlight to a tapered tip. It makes the top look rather like a metal bivouac that protects the regal occupants from the elements. Taut yet elegant surfaces exude a friendly look, while head and tail lamps that are small by SUV norms imbue the FX45 with a decidedly carlike image. As with the Murano, a high waistline but relatively shallow windows put the visual emphasis on the bulging wheelarches and scalloped bodyside and door profiles. Unlike the Murano, the FX45 sticks with a relatively subtle chrome slatted radiator grille, and also offers a V8 engine option. The interiors of both vehicles are simply executed, sparing of clutter, and heavy with aluminum detail, and present

a cosseting environment that would be decidedly alien to any Patrol devotee.

Interestingly, these two cars were intended for US consumption, but strong demand from Europe has forced Nissan to change its mind, on the Murano at least. With a global rollout of Infiniti in the early planning stages (in 2005), the FX45 could well be the stylish spearhead for a make that will be entirely new to the continent.

From just about any aspect, the Infiniti FX45 oozes presence, with its huge wheels seemingly pulling the close-fitting bodywork outward. It is at present sold only in the USA, where it outshines the output of many domestic manufacturers.

Chrysler Pacifica

If the sport utility vehicle itself is a construct of car types, then the Chrysler Pacifica takes the SUV idea and blurs it further by merging it with the best attributes of the multipurpose vehicle (MPV). This is something that had long been heralded as the next step in the SUV design pantheon, but DaimlerChrysler has actually been first to get such a product on to the road. The firm, however, is studiously avoiding any more acronyms for the Pacifica, instead christening it the world's first "sports tourer" and equating the importance of its introduction to the launch of the Chrysler Minivan series, the Dodge Caravan/Plymouth Voyager/Chrysler Town & Country, which galvanized the MPV into a customer-friendly form back in 1983.

DaimlerChrysler, however, also encompasses Jeep, which was absorbed into Chrysler in 1987, and the seed for the Pacifica was actually germinated in 1991 with the Jeep Wagoneer 2000 concept. This was a smooth-lined station wagon with an abnormally long

wheelbase, minimal front and rear overhangs, and three pairs of luxurious seats in a row, yet which also had excellent ground clearance for off-road ability—notionally at least, if not in real life, where the vehicle was a nonfunctioning styling exercise. Clearly it was felt by managers that such a crossover car would not be appropriate for the Jeep brand, but as an upmarket Chrysler it could carve a new niche for itself.

Led by Trevor Creed, a British designer of long standing at Chrysler, the Pacifica is smooth and wedge-shaped in its overall profile, all its styling lines fanning out and upward from a boldly chromed crisscross grille, while a barrel-sided body and a relatively narrow glasshouse give the car an aura of portly prosperity and easy comfort. Still, there are

Just as the Chrysler Minivan kick-started the MPV market in 1983, so twenty years later the Pacifica is changing the way Americans think about large family cars. The 2002 concept is shown above and opposite, the production car right.

none of the usual SUV visual trademarks designed to indicate that there is a four-wheel drive drivetrain beneath. An impression of ride height is given by black-painted lower panels rather than a gaping chasm between floorpan and road surface, while a low-slung front airdam and unadorned wheelarches do not indicate a relish for bouncing over boulders. The tapering windows and slim, horizontal door handles positioned along the very cusp of the car's waistline all boost a sleek image, with none of the rugged uprightness of, say, a Jeep Liberty.

The project cost just under $1,000,000,000 to develop, and was initiated in early 2000. In January 2002, the Pacifica was shown at the

Detroit Motor Show thinly disguised as a concept car but, in reality, ready to roll: just four months later, at the opening of the New York event, it was on sale. There were only tiny detail differences between the two vehicles in headlamps and door furnishing, plus wheels very slightly reduced in diameter—another sure sign that this car aims to catch intrigued customers from all walks of large-car life. A low step-in height and a powered tailgate must, after all, be designed to please those American buyers who are on the large side of unathletic.

Still, the Pacifica is something of a gamble, continuing Chrysler's reputation for taking design risks with its production cars—and making Ford and General Motors look very stick-in-the-mud. "Every year, more than 2.7 million people move in and out of sport utility vehicles, minivans, and sedans, which provides a great opportunity for Pacifica because of its unique design and high level of flexibility," said Tom Marinelli, vice president of Chrysler Marketing. "With innovative packaging, proportions and performance, Pacifica will offer a fresh alternative for people coming out of these traditional market segments," he continued

Fortunately, buyers love the Pacifica. Sourced from the company's Canadian plant in Windsor, more than 7500 vehicles a month were finding delighted new owners by September 2004 as sales snowballed and beat even those of the Volvo XC90 and Lexus RX300. To a Detroit "establishment" brand used to losing sales to trendy, design-conscious imports, this is some of the best news in years—especially for a company that, via its stewardship of Jeep, set the whole SUV phenomenon going more than sixty years ago.

The Pacifica is primarily an on-road vehicle, but it possesses both "sport" and "utility" by the bucketload. The car proves that the USA is more than capable of producing trendsetting designs in the face of fierce Japanese and European competition. The concept is shown right; the other images show the production version.

Glossary

It would be wrong to assume that every SUV owner, or student, would recognize all of the technical terms used in this book. So here they are, explained:

A-, B-, C-, and D-PILLARS

Vertical roof support posts that form parts of a car's bodywork. Moving rearward, the A-pillar sits between windshield and front door; the B-pillar between front and rear doors; the C-pillar between rear doors and rear window, hatchback, or wagon rear side windows; and D-pillar (on a wagon) between rear side windows and tailgate. Confusingly, however, some refer to the central pillar between front and rear doors as a B-pillar where it faces the front door and a C-pillar where it faces the rear one.

AIRDAM

A metal or plastic "lip" at the lowest point of the front of a car that improves aerodynamics by stopping moving air from getting underneath, reducing drag and lift, and so making the vehicle more stable.

ALL-WHEEL DRIVE

A permanently engaged or else automatically engaging four-wheel drive system; the driver does not choose the four-wheel drive mode because either the car supplies it constantly or else computer-controlled, sensor-activated equipment turns it on when it is required.

AXLE

Dictionary definitions give this as a pin or rod on the end of which a wheel rotates, and that is what it is in basic form on cars, located in place by the suspension system.

BHP

An acronym for "brake horsepower," an "Imperial" standard measurement of engine power that is gradually being replaced by a measure given in metric kilowatts (Kw). Both are calculated at optimum engine crankshaft speed, given in "rpm" (revolutions per minute) by manufacturers as a "net" measurement—an engine's output after power has been sapped by other equipment and the exhaust system—and measured by a "brake" applied to the driveshaft.

B-PILLAR

See A-, B-, C-, and D-PILLARS

B-POST

See A-, B-, C-, and D-PILLARS

BULLBAR

A generally tubular metal frame attached to the front of a car that is designed to protect its bodywork and structure from light accidental impact. In markets with highly developed legislation, bullbars tend to be fitted as "aftermarket" accessories because they would otherwise infringe construction regulations; such bars, while ideal for repelling straying beasts, can cause injuries to pedestrians that would not otherwise be sustained.

CANT RAIL

The roof frame section that runs longitudinally above the tops of the doors.

CHASSIS

The structural, load-bearing frame on which a vehicle is constructed, the chassis carries the mechanical components and acts as a support for the bodywork and its frame. The word has, in modern times, also come to mean a monocoque-construction car's drivetrain package and/or rolling floorpan, especially where this is shared with several other models. The final "s" is always silent except for the plural, which has the same spelling.

COIL-SPRUNG CHASSIS

A chassis in which the springing to cushion the impact between wheels and road surface is by means of steel coils.

CONCEPT CAR

Concept cars are not meant to be bought and driven by the public. They are intended to pave the way for future production models, often "softening the blow" of radical bodywork design changes to come. Or else they grab the media spotlight at motor shows when a manufacturer hits a spell of inactivity on the real new car front. They are the most glamorous part of the car industry's marketing process. The idea came from America, where, in 1933, the Briggs Body Company's design for an advanced rear-engined family car was the first. Today, Smart remains the only brand that has never exhibited a concept car.

COUPÉ

From the French *couper* for "cut." In horsedrawn coachbuilding, the term applied to the part of the carriage between the front "box" and the rear "trunk," or "boot." The term has evolved to mean two- or four-seater bodywork that has been stylishly foreshortened or cut back. Coupés can have two or four doors.

C-PILLAR

See A-, B-, C-, and D-PILLARS

DOUBLE-WISHBONE SUSPENSION

See WISHBONE SUSPENSION

D-PILLAR

See A-, B-, C-, and D-PILLARS

DRIVESHAFT

The revolving shaft that takes power from the engine to the wheels.

DRIVETRAIN

The assembly of "organs" that gives a car motive power: engine, gearbox, driveshaft, wheels, brakes, suspension, and steering. This lot is also known, loosely, these days as a chassis, and can be transplanted into several different models to save on development costs.

DRIVETRAIN SHIELD

A robust protective panel fitted to the underside of a car, to prevent damage to its components when traversing uneven ground.

FENDERLINE

The leading edge established at the corner of the front of a car by the fender/hood section, whose line is then carried back into the styling of the rest of the vehicle; its route can vary from halfway down the door panels to a diagonal route up and along the A-pillars.

FIELD CAR

A term originally coined by BBC radio and TV announcers in the 1950s to describe a Land Rover; "field car" was used to avoid breaking a BBC rule about not mentioning brand names.

FLOORPAN

A shallow pressed metal tray that forms the underside of the car. Clever design means the same floorpan, which carries suspension and other drivetrain, can be used for several different models.

FOUR-WHEEL DRIVE

A manually engaging, part-time system in which the car mostly uses two-wheel drive but can be switched to four as and when conditions demand.

FUEL INJECTION

A fuel supply system that does away with a carburetor and is universal to new cars. Gas is pumped, electrically, from the tank and sprayed straight into the engine's inlet ports, where it mixes with air before being burned in the cylinder. On diesel and direct-injection gas engines, fuel is injected into the cylinder rather than the inlet port.

GLASSHOUSE

The glazed upper part of the passenger cabin comprising the roof and windows, which are sometimes called the "daylight openings" by car designers.

GRAB HANDLE

A handle, fitted to the interior, that passengers can use to steady themselves when the car traverses rough terrain.

GRILLE

The slatted opening at the front of the car that generally serves as an air intake to cool the engine; often made from chrome-plated metal, differently shaped grilles have long served as identifying design features because they represent the centerpiece of cars' "faces."

HOT ROD

A term for any car whose performance has been increased by stripping away nonessential parts and boosting engine power.

LADDER FRAME/LADDER-FRAME CHASSIS

A chassis laid out with two longitudinal sidemembers connected by a series of crossmembers; the effect, in plan view, is of a ladder.

LEAF SPRING/LEAF-SPRING
A spring made up of narrow, curved metal strips of increasing length. Leaf springs are seen as old-fashioned but are notable for their toughness. The term also refers to a chassis' suspension system with leaf springs to cushion the impact between wheels and road surface.

MONOCOQUE
A car structure, now almost universal except among older SUV designs, in which the skin bears all the structural loads—effectively, the chassis and the body combined in one strong unit.

MPV
Short for Multi-Purpose Vehicle or Multi-Passenger Vehicle, it is usually applied to tall, spacious cars that can carry between five and eleven passengers, or else versatile combinations of people and cargo.

MULTILINK SUSPENSION
A complex and expensive suspension system in which additional linking parts are incorporated for optimum bump absorption while keeping the lateral movement of the car's structure to a minimum.

Nm
A measurement of force multiplied by distance to give a torque output. It is based on the physicist Sir Isaac Newton's "newton," the measurement of the force needed to accelerate a 1-kg object at a speed of one meter per second.

PRODUCTION CAR
Any car that is made to a set design in series, and offered for sale to the public at a catalog price.

ROOF BAR
A longitudinal bar, mounted on the car's roof, that can be used to secure a roof rack or luggage. Roof bars are often also designed to aid styling by drawing the eye along a horizontal plane.

RUNNING BOARD
An externally mounted ledge, fixed to the side of the car, on which people can step to gain access to the car, or else stand on to reach on to its roof.

SEDAN
Known in Britain as "saloon," this term usually means a car with two or four doors and a side profile that resembles three "boxes": a small box at the front housing the engine, a larger box in the center for the passengers, and a small box at the back for luggage.

SKID PAN TEST
A data-gathering procedure in which a car is subjected to violent handling maneuvers in a controlled environment. This is usually a smooth concrete or tarmac surface, often sprayed with water to simulate wet road conditions.

SOFT-ROADER
A derisory term for a four-wheel drive vehicle that, despite a utilitarian appearance, is designed primarily for on-road driving.

STATION WAGON
A boxy car with a large luggage-carrying capacity that can be increased by folding or removal of the rear seats. The title refers to the cars' use, in the early 20th century, on sheep stations in Australia and New Zealand, and also to the fact that they were used to ferry hotel guests to and from railway stations in 1920s America.

SUBFRAME
A type of bolt-on metal cradle in which two or more mechanical parts are carried in unison. The original Mini's is the most well-known example, because its engine, gearbox, and front-wheel drive units are contained in one assembly, and its rear suspension in another.

SUMP GUARD
A shield designed to protect the bottom of the engine from damage when the car is traversing rough terrain.

SUV
An acronym for Sport Utility Vehicle. Once confined to the car industry, the term has crossed over into everyday use.

SWAGE LINE
An emphatic design crease in a metal panel.

TAILGATE

The rear opening leading to the luggage compartment of a car in which the rear screen opens with the panel itself. Tailgates can swing open from the top or be split in two, with the top half hinged upward and the bottom half dropping downward.

TORQUE

Torque is, simply, the motion of twisting or turning. In car terms, it means, basically, pulling power, generated by twisting force from the crankshaft, and that is often necessary for working off-road vehicles. The better the torque, the more force the engine can apply to the driven wheels. Torque is measured in pounds feet or newton-meters.

TORSION BAR

A suspension component in the form of a steel bar that is fixed to the axle at one end and the body structure at the other, and acts as a spring when twisted by the car's movements.

TRANSFER CASE

A gearbox that distributes power to the front and rear axles of a four-wheel drive vehicle. Depending on the car, a transfer case may allow shifting between two-wheel drive, full-time four-wheel drive, part-time four-wheel drive, and low-range four-wheel drive.

TURBOCHARGER

A device that boosts engine power, a turbocharger uses waste exhaust gases to drive a turbine that forces air into the combustion chambers, in turn increasing the throughput and, so, the power available. A supercharger, by contrast, uses an engine-driven compressor to do the same thing.

TURBODIESEL

A turbocharged diesel engine.

TWIN-CAM ENGINE

An engine with two camshafts.

UNDERFRAME

The underframe is the outer profile of the floorpan and, unless aerodynamically designed as in the McLaren F1 supercar, is usually an unsightly mass of steel crimpings, joins, bumps, and alcoves to accommodate external fittings such as the exhaust system.

V8 ENGINE

An engine with its cylinders arranged in a V-formation, with four on either side; there have been V4, V6, V8, V10, V12, and V16 configurations. This format makes for the most compact engines, explaining why in-line engines of more than four cylinders are rare today; an in-line 12, for instance, would require a very long hood. Only Volkswagen makes a W12, an engine with its 12 cylinders arranged in a W-formation.

V10 ENGINE

See V8 ENGINE

V12 ENGINE

See V8 ENGINE

VALANCE

An apron at the front or back of a car that is often used to conceal the join between chassis and body, as well as neatly carrying items such as lights and number plate mounting recesses.

WHEELBASE

The exact distance between the center of the front wheel and center of the rear wheel.

WHITEWALL TIRES

No longer fashionable, these are tires with a circular strip of white rubber inlaid on their walls for decorative effect.

WISHBONE SUSPENSION

A suspension link, shaped like the wishbone of a chicken, formed like a letter A. The wheel and its hub carrier are attached to the apex of this A, while the two spaced-out arms of the link pivot from their attachment to the car's main structure. Double-wishbone suspension, with a shorter upper wishbone and a slightly longer lower one, is a system known to give good suspension geometry, resulting in well-controlled road behavior.

Page numbers in **bold** indicate main references; page numbers in *italics* refer to illustrations.

A

Alfa Romeo 1900M **48–49**, *50*
"all-wheel drive" 16–17
AM General Corporation 216
American Bantam Car Company 32, 34
American Motors 216
American Motors Javelin 90
Aneiros, Rick 21–23, *27*
Asensio, Anne 190
Audi (company) 96
Audi allroad quattro **188–90**
Audi quattro 15, *18*
AutoVaz 116, 118

B

Bache, David 76
Barker, Tony 42
Bashford, Gordon 76
Bertone, Nuccio 72
Bertone Freeclimber *144*, 147
Blackett, Tom 143
Blitz Buggy 32, 34–35
BMW X3 20, **186–87**
BMW X5 18, **184–86**, 215
British Motor Corporation 69

C

Cadillac Escalade **204–206**
Cadillac Evoq roadster concept 207
Cadillac SRX **206–207**
Callum, Ian 220
Cappy, Joseph 128
Castaing, François 120–21, 122, 123
Chevrolet Blazer 60, 63, **84–87**
Chevrolet/GMC Suburban **64–67**
Chevrolet Tahoe 84, 202
Chrysler Minivan 228, *229*
Chrysler Pacifica **228–31**

Chrysler PT Cruiser 200
Citroën Mehari 68, *69*, **70**
Cox, Simon *156*, 158–59
Creed, Trevor 229

D

Daihatsu Feroza 18, **144–47**
Daihatsu Fourtrak 144
Daihatsu Rocky 144, *145*, 147
Daihatsu Sportrak 18, 144, *145*, 147, *147*, 168
Daihatsu Taft *80*, **82–83**
Daihatsu Terios **83**
DaimlerChrysler 21, 228
Dangel, Automobiles 134
DKW Munga 96
Dodge Dakota 200, *202*
Dodge Durango **200–203**
Dodge Ram pickup 200, *203*
Dodge Viper 200

F

Farina, Battista "Pinin" 72
Fiat Campagnola 48, *48*, **49–50**, *51*
Fiat Panda 4x4 **132–33**
Fissore 72
Fissore Scout **72–74**
Ford (company) 15, 34, 78, 204, 206
Ford Baja Bronco 60
Ford Bronco **60–63**, 86, 148
Ford Cortina MkIII 90
Ford Escape 25
Ford Expedition 204
Ford Explorer 25, **136–39**, 152, 202
Ford Freestyle 27, *29*
Ford General Purpose (GP) 32, 34, 35
Ford Ka 156
Ford Maverick 172, **174–75**
Ford Tempo 17
"four-by-fours" 12
"four-wheel drives" 12, 16, 235
Frey, Donald 60
FWD *11*, 12

G

General Motors 15, *22*, 148, 192, 204, 216, 218
Giugiaro, Giorgetto 132
GMC Jimmy 80, 84, 86
GMC Suburban **64–67**
GMC Yukon 66
Goudie, Andrew 25
Grade, Anthony 190
Greenley, Ken 152–53

H

Heffernan, John 152
Honda CR-V **164**, *165*, 167
Honda HR-V **164–65**, *166*
Honda Passport 113
Honda Pilot **166–67**
Horbury, Peter 212, 214
Hummer H1 17, *22*, 94, **216–19**
Hummer H2 *22*, 218
Hyundai Santa Fe **196–99**
Hyundai Tucson **198–99**

I

IDEA Institute 173–74
Infiniti FX45 20, 207, 224, **226–27**
International Harvester Company 52
International Scout *9*, 10, **52–55**, 92
Issigonis, Alec 68
Isuzu Amigo **112–15**, 172
Isuzu MU 112, 113
Isuzu Rodeo 113, 164
Isuzu Trooper *112*, **114**, 142
Isuzu Unicab 114, *114*
Isuzu VehiCROSS 18, *24*, **156–59**

J

Jeep 21–23, 35, 39
see also Willys Jeep
Jeep Cherokee 16, 18, *19*, 59, 86, **120–23**, 136
Jeep CJ7 128

Jeep Grand Cherokee 22, *122*, **123**, 202
Jeep Rescue concept 23, *27*
Jeep Treo concept 23, *28*
Jeep Wagoneer 14–15, *15*, **56–59**, 60, 92, 120, 228
Jeep Wrangler 22, **128–31**
Jensen FF 15, *16*, 88
Jones, Parnelli 60

K

Kia Sorento *152*, *153*, **154**
Kia Sportage **153–54**, *155*
King, Spencer 76
Koizumi, Iwao 21

L

Lada Niva **116–19**
LaForza *126*, 127
Lamborghini Cheetah 93–94
Lamborghini LM *93*, **94–95**
Land Rover (company) 15, 76
Land Rover Defender 40, 42, *43*, 180, 143
Land Rover Discovery 42, **140–43**, 164
Land Rover Freelander 42, 143, 164, **180–83**
Land Rover Series I 13, *13*, **40–42**
Land Rover Series II 42, *42*
Land Rover Series III 42, *43*
Lawes, Major H.J. 34
le Quément, Patrick 190, *191*
Lexus RX300 20, *25*, 167, **208–11**, 231
Lincoln Navigator **204–206**
Loewy, Raymond 36
Löhner-Porsche 12, *12*
Lunn, Roy 120, 121, 122
Lutz, Bob 200, 202

M

McGovern, Gerry 180, 182, *182*
Maina, Franco 74
Malvino, Giuliano 124
Mantegazza, Franco 174

Manx *see* Meyers Manx
Marshall, General George 35
Matra Rancho **100–103**
Mazda MX-Crossport 20–21, *26*
Mazda RX-01 21
Mercedes-Benz Geländewagen
    (G-Wagen) 18, **98–99**
Mercedes-Benz M-Class **160–63**,
    167, 208
Mercedes-Benz SLK 156
Meyers, Bruce 18
Meyers Manx 18–19
Mini Moke **68–70**
Mitsubishi Pajero 18, 83, **108–11**,
    142, 196
Mitsubishi Pajero Evolution 2+2
    20
Mitsubishi Pajero MkII *23*,
    109, *111*
Monteverdi, Peter 77, 92, 93
Monteverdi Safari **92–93**
Moretti 72
Moretti MidiMaxi *72*, **74–75**
Murayama, Satomi 158

N

Nesbitt, Dick 63
Nissan (company) 15
Nissan Murano **224–25**
Nissan Patrol **104–107**
Nissan Terrano **106**, *107*
Nissan Terrano II **172–74**
Niva *see* Lada Niva
Nonaka, Masakatu 168, 171

O

"off-roaders" 12
Opel Frontera 113, *115*
O'Rourke, P.J. 28, *28*
Oshawa, Hiroshi 46

P

Paluch, Frank 166
Pearce, Harry 207
Peugeot 405 134
Peugeot 505 Dangel **134–35**

Pininfarina 50, *51*, 124
Plymouth Prowler 200
Pontiac Aztek **192–95**
Porsche Cayenne 215, **220–22**
Probst, Karl 34

R

Range Rover 17, *21*, 26, **76–79**, 92
Rayton Fissore Magnum 48,
    124–27
Renault Megane Scenic 4X4
    190–91
Renault Rodeo **70**
Roos, Delmar "Barney" 32, 35
Royal College of Art, London 29,
    152, 158, 212

S

Sancer, Derek 196
Savio 72
Savio Jungla **72**, *74*
Shanghai Automotive Industry
    Corporation 155
Simca 100, 102
Sorensen, Charles 36, 38
Spyker 12
SsangYong Musso **152–53**
SsangYong Rexton *154*, **155**
Stevens, Brooks 13, 14, *14*, 36, 38,
    39, *59*
Steyr-Daimler-Puch 132
Steyr-Daimler-Puch Haflinger 132
Stoppe, Bill 60
Subaru Forester 25, 90, **176–79**
Subaru Impreza 90, 178
Subaru Justy 17, 133
Subaru Leone 15, *17*, **88–91**
SUV: definition 9–12
Suzuki Jimny **80–82**, *83*
Suzuki Vitara 147, **148**, *149*, *150*,
    151, 168, 172
Suzuki X-90 **148–51**, 156

T

Taira, Ichiro 44
Teague, Walter Dorwin 36

Tjaarda, John 124
Tjaarda, Tom 124, *125*, 127
Touring, Carrozzeria, of Milan *16*
Toyota (company) 15
Toyota Harrier 208
Toyota Land Cruiser 25, **44–47**, 80,
    142, 208
Toyota Prius 25
Toyota RAV4 16, 18, *20*, **168–71**

U

Umehara, Hanji 44

V

Vauxhall Frontera 113
Volanis, Antoine 100
Volkswagen Golf Country **133–34**
Volkswagen Golf Syncro 133
Volkswagen Iltis **96–98**
Volkswagen 181 ("The Thing")
    70–71
Volkswagen Touareg 20, **222–23**
Volvo PV444 212
Volvo XC90 **212–15**, 231

W

Wagner, Thomas 138–39
Warkuss, Hartmut 222
Wilks, Maurice and Spencer 40,
    42
Willys Jeep 12, 13–14, **32–35**, 39,
    108, 216
    CJ3B *35*
    CJ5 *32*
    MA *34*
    MB *33*
    see also Jeep
Willys Jeep Station Wagon **36–39**
Willys Jeepster 14, *14*, **38–39**
Willys-Overland 32, 34, 35
    General Purpose vehicles
        10, 32
    Quad 32, 34–35
    see also Willys Jeep;
        Willys Jeepster

The illustrations in this book have been reproduced courtesy of the following copyright holders:

Alamy: 21, 22, 23, 24; **Alfa Romeo:** 48, 49t, 49b, 50t, 50b, 51bl; **Audi:** 188, 189t, 189b; **BMW:** Jacket, front br, 184, 185t, 185bl, 185br, 186, 187t, 187bl, 187br; **British Motor Industry Heritage Trust:** 41b, 43cr, 76cr, 76br, 77b, 141bl, 182b, 183b; **Neill Bruce:** 27, 28, 52, 175, 216; **Giles Chapman:** 11, 12, 16, 17, 18, 19, 25, 40, 44, 62, 73, 74, 75, 80, 82, 83, 88, 89t, 89b, 90–91, 90b, 91b, 92, 102t, 102b, 104, 106b, 107b, 109b, 112, 113, 114, 115, 116, 117t, 118t, 119t, 120, 126t, 126b, 127t, 127b, 135, 138t, 138b, 139t, 139b, 140b, 144t, 144b, 145t, 145b, 147t, 148, 149t, 149b, 150t, 157t, 158, 159cr, 159b, 160, 165t, 165b, 169b, 170b, 173b, 174, 199t, 200, 201b, 202t, 202b, 203t, 203b, 208, 209t, 209b, 217t, 217b, 218, 219t, 219b; **Chrysler:** Jacket, back cr, 15, 32, 33, 34t, 34b, 35t, 35b, 36, 37, 38, 39, 56, 57t, 57b, 58t, 58b, 59t, 59b, 121t, 121b, 122t, 122b, 123t, 123b, 128, 129t, 129bl, 129br, 130t, 130b, 131t, 131b, 201t, 228t, 228b, 229t, 229b, 230t, 230b, 231t, 231b; **Citroën:** 69tl, 69tr, 69cl, 69b; **Corbis:** 10; **Fiat:** 51t, 51br, 132, 133t, 133b; **Ford:** Jacket, front bc, 29, 61t, 204, 205t, 205b; **General Motors:** 64t, 64b, 65t, 65b, 66t, 66b, 67t, 67b, 84, 85t, 85cr, 85bl, 85br, 86t, 86bl, 86br, 87t, 87b, 192, 193, 194, 195, 206t, 206b, 207; **Honda:** 166t, 166b, 167t, 167b; **Hyundai:** 196, 197t, 197b; **Infiniti News:** 224, 226t, 226b, 227t, 227b; **Kia:** 152, 153b; **Lamborghini:** 94l, 94r, 95t, 95b; **Land Rover:** Jacket, back cl, 41t, 42, 43t, 43bl, 76bl, 77t, 78–79, 78t, 78b, 140t, 141t, 141br, 142t, 142b, 143t, 143b, 180, 181t, 181b, 182t, 183t; **LAT Photographic:** 90b; **Mercedes:** 96b, 97, 98t, 98b, 99, 161t, 161b, 162t, 162b, 163t, 163b; **Mitsubishi:** Jacket, back b, 108, 109tl, 109tr, 110t, 110b, 111tl, 111tr, 111bl; **National Motor Museum, Beaulieu:** 13, 14, 26, 60, 61b, 63t, 63b, 68, 93t, 93b, 100–101, 100b, 101b, 103, 107t, 111br, 117b, 118b, 119b, 124, 125t, 125bl, 125br, 136, 137, 146t, 146b, 153t, 156, 157b, 164, 168, 169t, 170t, 171t, 171b, 178b, 179b, 210, 211t, 211b; **Newspress:** 81, 147b, 154t, 154b, 155t, 155b, 176, 177t, 177b, 178t, 179t, 198t, 198b, 199b; **Nissan:** Jacket, back tr, 105t, 105b, 106t, 172t, 172b, 173t, 225t, 225bl, 225br; **Porsche:** Jacket, front t, 220t, 220b, 221t, 221b; **Renault:** 70t, 70cl, 70cr, 190, 191t, 191b; **Scout Connection:** 9, 55b; **Suzuki:** 83, 150b, 151; **Toyota:** Jacket, back tl, 20, 45b, 45cr, 46, 47tl, 47tr, 47b; **Volkswagen:** 71t, 71b, 96t, 134, 222t, 222b, 223t, 223b; **Volvo:** Jacket, front bl, 212, 213t, 213b, 214t, 214b, 215t, 215b; **Wisconsin Historical Trust:** 53, 54, 55t.

The publisher has made every effort to trace and contact copyright holders of the illustrations reproduced in this book; we will be happy to correct in subsequent editions any errors or omissions that are brought to our attention.